101

TOP TIPS

for

PRIMARY TEACHERS

MORE THAN

101

TOP TIPS

for

PRIMARY TEACHERS

Steve Gibson

British Library Cataloguing in Publication Data. A catalogue record for this book is available from the British Library

Contents

Introduction

*There is time and space in the
school day and in each week, term
and year to range beyond the
national curriculum specifications.*

(National Curriculum 2010 Section 3.2)

The 2010 National Curriculum has the audacity to include this sentence. Any teacher working in any school in the country knows that the school day is absolutely packed... And yet...

With the determination of the captain of the Titanic seeking to beat his deadline, I decided to look at every aspect of my practice and see if I could streamline my workload. What shocked me most was that, instead of failing as I'd expected, I succeeded!

A teacher is a bit like a plate spinner trying to keep as many plates spinning as possible before one drops. I realised fairly quickly that the art of teaching is knowing which plates NOT to spin. It is impossible to do everything 100% perfectly correct every time, but if we quickly identify those areas that increase progress within the class, or equip them to learn more efficiently, then we give them the chance to make the most of their education.

I also discovered lots of small changes that could be made that saved me time and allowed me to spin more plates.

I began to introduce some of these top tips to my teacher training lectures and, unsurprisingly, discovered that the only notes the students actually took were my top tips! They didn't care about the Computing subject matter – they wanted real-life examples of good practice to try for themselves so that they could become better teachers.

This book is a collection of those top tips. Some will be so obvious you'll wonder why you never thought of them. Some just won't fit your style of teaching – if that's the case, don't use them! Be the best teacher YOU can be and come up with your own solutions. Some will be things you've always done and didn't realise others needed to know about them.

Whatever is true, share these ideas. Talk to your teams. Try things out and discover creative ways to give your class the best possible start in life, and memories that will last a lifetime.

As I was writing this book, I reached out to a group of teaching assistants for any top tips. Remember, they spend time working with a variety of teachers but also work closely with children in a way we often can't as class teachers.

They are also your most important resource – they will have an opportunity to get to know the children in a way you don't, working closely with small groups. They have ideas that are just as valuable as any expert! I valued my teaching assistants as virtual equals and expected my class to treat them with absolute respect too.

Partner with your teaching assistants. Invent in them. Model the practice you expect, and if you believe they aren't doing what you expect, decide whether it was your unclear instructions, a misunderstanding, or lack of training. Resource them. Give them the tools they need to be able to work on top form. They are incredibly underpaid, over skilled individuals with experience that can make a huge difference to the children in your class.

I wish you well as you strive to improve the educational experience for those in your care. When things seem like they will overwhelm you (which they inevitably will around report-writing time), remember this quote from Mother Theresa:

Yesterday has gone,
Tomorrow has not yet come.
We only have today,
Let us begin.

1

General Tips

MAKE MEMORIES

I was working in a secondary school and bumped into a past pupil, now in Year 10. He looked at me, confused, then said, "You were my Year 5 teacher." Next, he turned to his friends and said, "He introduced us to Rubik's cubes and Clash Royale." His first thoughts weren't curriculum-linked – his memories were the little extras that made the classroom special. Through Clash Royale we'd learnt about community, maths (through comparing stats of cards) and teamwork. Through Rubik's cube we'd learnt about algorithms, developing patience as those that knew taught those that didn't, and some people even learned their left and right! Everything was an exciting opportunity to learn; the world was full of wonder. That's what this secondary school pupil remembered the most.

CHEATING IS GOOD, UNLESS IT'S NOT

Children are taught very early on that cheating is wrong, especially copying from somebody else. However, we also know that when we explain a concept to somebody else, it can help refine their understanding. I used to encourage my class to 'cheat' – but they weren't allowed to copy unless they understood what they were copying. This legitimised collaboration instantly.

This only works if you form a supportive class atmosphere focused on respect. Children need to be encouraged to help each other and 'travel together.' There are many learning models that say that when you can explain something to somebody else, you truly understand it. I described it as 'cheating' to my class because it sounds naughtier, but it's basically allowing them to verbalise their learning in a way that enables their peers to increase their level of progress.

This is also particularly useful for those children who are verbal processors. These children can frustrate teachers as they learn best when they speak out loud – the opposite of the calm (or silent) classroom we are often encouraged to foster. By allowing time to discuss possible answers, those children also have the opportunity to process their problems verbally.

PAUSE BEFORE YOU SPEAK

If you have ever watched a reality show on TV, you'll know there is a moment when the presenters pause before revealing the results of the latest phone vote. This carefully timed pause is just long enough to feel uncomfortable – around ten seconds. Try counting in your head as you watch and you'll find it is usually the same length, regardless of programme.

In normal circumstances, when there is this level of awkwardness, people feel the need to fill the silence. This is useful for several reasons.

First, when asking somebody about a behavioural situation, pausing may lead them to reveal more information that they would otherwise have hidden. The awkward silence is filled with a fresh revelation or confession.

Second, some children NEED the pause. My own son, a verbal processor, used to ask questions out loud when doing group work. Adults nearby would perceive this as a request for help and answer him. Eventually, he formed the bad habit of asking things out loud and not even starting to think, knowing somebody would provide the answer. Another child I taught used to say "I don't know" before then giving me the answer. The first time she did this, it caught me out and I jumped in to help. The second time, I caught myself, paused, and she proceeded to give me the correct solution despite her initial claim!

LET CHILDREN CHOOSE THEIR ACTIVITIES

After the teaching input, provide a series of different possible activities for children to complete, ranked in order of difficulty. Allow the children the option of choosing where they start, depending on their confidence level. You might be surprised by what they choose!

Also encourage them to self-assess their progress, deciding when they're ready for the next activity. If it's not hard enough, they can move on to the next activity as soon as they are ready, sometimes without even completing the rest of the questions. It can sometimes be useful to have an 'exit' question that they have to get right before they move on.

From a child's point of view, there is nothing worse than being stuck answering 20 very similar questions when they've mastered the skill and want to move on. It's a complete waste of their energy. I used to encourage my class to skip questions in order to get to meatier work. There was no such thing as a slow lane – if somebody understood something, they moved on.

To quote a child from a friend's class, "if we get all the questions right, we haven't chosen an activity that challenged us enough." She had set the expectation that we should be challenging and pushing ourselves, and the children had embraced it fully.

DISTRACTIONS ARE YOUR FRIEND

Bluma Zeigarnik conducted research into memory and

interruptions back in 1927[1]. He discovered that when our mind is distracted and then returns to a topic, it is more likely to remember it. Our short-term memory takes in lots of information and forgets most of it. It's why we forget why we went upstairs, for example.

During intervention groups, adding in a quick distraction can allow the children to lose track of where they are so that they can be brought back on task later. This enables their short-term memory to recognise that the knowledge being imparted is important. This is the same principle that proves homework can be useful – it is in returning to a topic that our memory realises it is important enough to remember for longer.

MAKE PAPER AEROPLANES

Nothing makes an activity less attractive than turning it into a real lesson. Encourage children to make different planes, including creative designs. They'll be following instructions carefully, which is a great skill in itself. You could even ask them to refine the instructions. Try to include those paper planes that look like cylinders – they're totally impractical for real life but do fly further than most traditional plane shapes. Discuss the forces acting on the plane, the impact of friction, compare them to real-life designs.

---

1   https://en.wikipedia.org/wiki/Zeigarnik_effect

BE PUNNY

I still remember a lesson on rocks led by a local secondary school. I went around like a naughty school child telling various puns: "this rocks" or "barely scratched the surface" or "HARDly touched that one..." They got worse and worse as I thought of more that related to the core vocabulary. When it came to the test, my class beat my neighbours' class easily. They remembered the puns, even if they groaned the whole way through.

Litter your lessons with puns. They don't have to be great – just bad enough to keep children's attention and stick in the mind. In the Autumn term the class would laugh with me, in the Spring term they would laugh at me, and in the Summer term they'd groan. But parents still reported hearing all the jokes when they got home...

ECHO KEYWORDS AND PHRASES

Photosynthesis: the first scientific word most people learn that sounds posh enough to show off to others. But in modern primary teaching there is a lot more complicated terminology that we need children to understand in order to demonstrate their skills in assessments.

I would make fun out of those keywords. 'Algorithm' is a great word used in computing that essentially means 'instruction.' Every time I used the word 'algorithm', I would repeat it three times, each time in a slightly different voice. Or I would make it sound like an echo, getting quieter each time.

It became a fun thing for children to look out for and helped them remember the core vocabulary; they associated it with a happy or silly moment, embedding it in their memory more easily.

REMAIN NEUTRAL

It is not your job to tell your class what to believe, or which political party they should follow. Your job is to present them with unbiased facts and encourage them to respectfully consider and discuss different viewpoints. I have been dismayed when observing Religious Studies lessons to find people using language such as 'we' and 'they' instead of the correct terminology. For example, when a guest comes in to speak about their faith, I heard a teacher ask, "What do you Christians believe that we don't believe?" In another scenario, during a talk from a religious leader, the teacher interrupted to define faith as 'something people make up when they don't understand something.'

If your child was taught by someone with differing views to your own, you would want assurances that they were teaching in a neutral manner, so please, please do the same. By all means, encourage debate, but instead of 'them and us' talk

CASE STUDY

In one lesson, I wanted to introduce my Year 3 class to a story writing unit based on monsters. I wanted them to consider the emotions involved. If I had told them this at the very start, they would not have enjoyed my starter. First, I sat down as if to start the lesson and began to say, "today's objective..." but then stopped and asked, "did you hear something?" They all listened and said no. We started again and I stopped again. We decided to investigate – the class knew we were about to go on a mini-adventure. I love the imagination of children when it is allowed to go wild!

We all crept – 30 children, two teaching assistants and me – out of the classroom and towards the staff room nearby. I paused for effect several times. We got close to the door. I slowly put my hand out. A third teaching assistant who had been lying in wait started to open the staff room door, and a cuddly toy monster's hand appeared in the gap followed by a growling sound. I turned to my class and said "monster! – shh – don't let it know we're here. Let's get back to the class!"

We ran (sensible walked quickly I think would be a more appropriate description to appear on the planning) back to the classroom and all hid under our desks. One child with a VERY active imagination held the hand of one of my teaching assistants (I was prepared for her overreaction). And then I said, "we're safe – how do you all feel?"

We began collecting the BEST selection of words relating to emotion, and the writing they did – based on a monster teacher hiding in the staffroom – was insane! If I had told them the objective, it would have spoiled everything.

about Muslims, Conservatives, Campaign Supporters... Talk about people groups with respect, and focus on the heart behind the actions. Why do Jews remember still celebrate Passover? So that they can express gratitude to God for the ways He has blessed them while ensuring that their cultural heritage is not forgotten. Dig deeper and remain neutral, and you'll soon discover your children have developed a new depth of compassion and understanding that might just transform society one day...

CASE STUDY

I was preparing to teach a lesson on the properties of water at different temperatures. I had already created an ice balloon (a balloon filled with water and frozen overnight to create a beautiful spherical ice cube) and prepared various other examples. At the end of the lesson, I pointed out we had no objective and asked the class to come up with something. They told *me* what they had learned and used the technical language they had picked up to create a really high-quality learning objective. Obviously, I filtered suggestions carefully to ensure they matched my own aims, but not knowing exactly what they were investigating beforehand helped them to 'discover' the learning objective contents for themselves, and broadened their thinking, giving them permission to learn beyond the limits of the objective.

START THE LESSON BY NOT SHARING THE OBJECTIVE

Nobody would watch *EastEnders* (or any other soap or drama) if all the plot twists had already been revealed. Although we all want to know the twist, it's MUCH more satisfying when it's revealed in the drama itself. The fun is in the anticipation.

Lessons can be the same.

Yes, there are times when sharing the objective will help focus the class. But there are other times when spoilers will ruin the success of your lesson.

2

Classroom Management

MANAGE YOUR STATIONARY

At the start of each year, I used to be given a stash of fresh stationery. I was told that this was my ration for the year. Most teachers put all the resources out for everyone to use, and by Easter were running short of glue sticks, had no red colouring pencils, and were begging and scrounging for a working whiteboard pen. In contrast, I always had enough of everything to last.

To achieve this, I split everything I was given into piles. Depending on what I had, this might be a pile for each term or a pile for each table group. In the perfect scenario, it would be both!

During class inspections, I'd check that everyone had looked after their resources (see *Class Inspections top tip*). Missing caps were easily replaced (see the *Award-winning Idea top tip*). Children knew how long things had to last. They were given responsibility and ownership of their resources.

When children see an abundance of resources – piles of glue sticks that seem to get replenished easily – they don't value them. They will consider that you as the teacher will provide, and when you don't, you have failed. Instead, if you give them their ration, they take responsibility. It's a small change in mindset, but it works.

PRODUCTIVE NOISE

Many children need to verbalise their thoughts. I've worked with many children who reveal their thought process by speaking them out loud. It's important to allow your class the opportunity to talk. Sometimes it may be suitable to provide discussion questions or conversation ladders. Why not walk around your class just listening to conversations? You can highlight good quality conversations or language, while also keeping an eye on potentially less productive chatter.

It's also a really nice phrase to be able to use when children are talking and the class is getting noisy. Rather than complain about the noise, you can thank children for their 'productive noise'. Often when I did this, the unproductive noise would stop. Children were fully aware I was using this as a passive-aggressive reminder to behave but responded well because they knew they weren't being directly told off.

DON'T BOTHER WRITING THE DATE ON THE BOARD

At the start of every day, every teacher changes the date on their board. Some are even more efficient, and do it before they leave the previous day. (That in itself might be the efficiency tip you need most.)

Why not only change the date on a Monday? After that, the class has to work out the date! This is a great mental exercise, saves you time and makes sure the class doesn't go into auto-drive and forget what they were supposed to be doing.

BAN PENCIL SHARPENING AT TABLES

This may seem tiny but focusing on tiny things raises awareness of big things. Explain to the class that the cleaner has to spend longer cleaning the class when they make it messy. We want to respect the cleaner by keeping our class tidy so that they can get on with their job.

Always sharpen pencils over the bin!

And have an expectation that if a child drops a pencil sharpening on the floor, it is picked up and put in the bin. Don't allow the floor around the bin to become messy either... Some children would have pencil sharpeners that contained the sharpenings inside – I would still insist on these being emptied into the bin, as they had a tendency to 'fall open' in the wrong hands.

EMBRACE THE AWARD-WINNING IDEA

Lids! Ever had a glue stick or pen that runs dry because the lid is missing? The solution is easy! Have a pot somewhere in your class for old pen and glue stick lids – or any other lid that might be useful. If children find a glue stick with no lid, they go straight to the pot and grab a spare. When the missing lid is found, it goes into the pot. This will save you a fortune!

Why is it an award-winning idea? I used to use an old, unmarked trophy that I found at a car boot sale as my pot to store the lids. And I'd joke with the class that it was a trophy because... it was an award-winning idea. It added to the novelty and children seemed to love the fact there was a trophy in the room.

HOLD REGULAR TABLE INSPECTIONS

At the end of messy lessons, and without fail at the end of every day, hold a table inspection. Explain that every table starts with 10 points, and for each mistake you find, one point will be lost. The table with the most points gets to leave the classroom first.

CASE STUDY

My class had lined up beautifully and I was about to take them in from lunch break to the classroom. At that particular school, packed lunch boxes were kept on a trolley and wheeled outside ready for lunchtime. In each class, somebody was responsible for wheeling them back inside.

But not in mine.

As we walked back in the class, one boy – diagnosed with ADHD and previously the 'naughty' child of the class – noticed that nobody was returning the lunch trolley. He left the line and walked over, taking the initiative and fixing the problem. At just 7 years old, he had realised he could make a difference without being asked.

It was at this point another teacher, who knew the poor reputation of the child, walked up. I overheard this conversation:

Teacher: Why are you pushing the trolley? Is it your job?

Child: Mr Gibson doesn't give us jobs.

Teacher: So why are you pushing it?

Child: It needed pushing.

Teacher: But Mr Gibson wouldn't trust YOU to push that trolley, surely?

I saw his face drop. At the start of the year, he'd considered himself a 'bad child' and I'd worked hard to change this. When ➔

➜ he returned to the class, I thanked him profusely and held him up as a good example.

When I stopped being his teacher, I asked him to describe himself. He no longer said, "I'm bad." Instead he replied, "I'm good, but sometimes I make mistakes." He had begun to see the potential of who he could be, because I put my faith in him, trusted him, praised him when he got it right and made sure that the attention he received was positive, not negative.

When you first start this, keep it simple. Choose something to focus on, like checking all their whiteboard pens have lids. After a while, you'll find you need to get fussier and fussier. My favourite was blunt pencils or a broken off pencil lead in the bottom of the container. I also made sure that there was the right number of everything on each table ready for the next lesson. There were trays at the front of the class with spare equipment that could be collected, but also if someone found they had too much, they would return the spares to the trays. It prevented people from stealing from other tables. If they were missing a ruler AND there were no spares, they wouldn't be penalised.

I would also casually add in responsibility for areas near their desks. I still remember the angry faces of a table who lost 5 points because there were 5 pencils UNDERNEATH the bookshelf BEHIND their table. (I'd spotted someone rolling one spare underneath to avoid losing a point.) I would also take points away if children spoke during an inspection, or had their shirts untucked. There was genuine pride in the class appearance, and this became a natural habit rather than an instruction over time.

DON'T HAVE CLASS MONITORS

There is a fad where every child is given responsibility for a particular part of keeping the class tidy. This is supposed to boost their confidence. However, there is a major problem with this. It absolves everyone else from responsibility for that thing. Ever heard someone say "it's not my job"? It's your fault! Instead, make everybody responsible for everything. They will suddenly become more aware of what needs doing...

POSE INSTRUCTIONS AS QUESTIONS

When children (or indeed adults) solve a multi-step problem, we go through an internal dialogue. This is rarely formed as instructions. We just don't say to ourselves, "First, lay out the jigsaw pieces. Next, find the edges." Instead, we tend to say, "Right, are all the pieces the right way up? No? Let's fix that. Okay. Where are the edges?"

We pose questions.

And yet when we give instructions for an activity, we write them as statements. If we write them as questions instead, then we begin training children to use this model of internal dialogue. Whether you're working with the whole class or a small group, constantly pose questions. If a child is stuck, pose questions to lead them towards understanding. When working with staff and providing support and training, continue to pose questions. This is a form of coaching, and rarely will you also have to answer your own question. Often, there is some level of understanding already present that can be extended.

These questions – often framed the same way over and over – became the internal dialogue that people need in order to learn the method/solve the problem effectively.

COLLECT BOOKS IN TABLES

I used to have magazine boxes for each table; one each for literacy and numeracy books. When I wanted to mark them, I kept them in tables. (It also cut marking down into manageable chunks and upped my step count.) When children wanted their books, they didn't have to wait for somebody to hand them out – they were already sorted by table.

Also, if somebody picked up the wrong book from the box, they wouldn't put it back. They would give it to the correct person. I once handed out a pile of topic books, giving every single one to the wrong person. They had to correct me and deliver it to the correct person. This ended up being faster than me walking around the class randomly, or even asking a small group of children to randomly hand out books!

If I ever did ask children to hand out books, I'd choose people based on the name on the top book. That way, the first one was already handed out. This saved a few seconds for that person, and for me too.

MAKE FIRE DRILLS MORE EFFICIENT

The dreaded fire drill has begun. Your class has lined up beautifully and is now outside. You are calling the register to make sure everybody is present. But so are all the other teachers. Every time you hear "Here" you're not sure if it's your class or not.

I have the perfect solution: echoed names. I trained my class so that during a fire drill, they would say their name instead of saying "here." When I heard their name echoed back, I'd know for sure it was them.

USE THE REGISTER TO LEARN PRONUNCIATION

When you take the register only say hello to the first person.

They say hello to the next person, etc, etc. The last person says hello to you, then you say hello to the whole class and they echo back. This may seem silly, but now when you ask the class to line up in register order, they'll do it easily. This also means that when they line up for a fire drill, they can be quickly lined up in alphabetical order with no fuss, which makes taking the register outside MUCH easier. Other staff will be in shock at your fire drill efficiency.

INTRODUCE A CHESS LEAGUE

I once inherited a class that was notoriously disengaged with learning. I used all sorts of gimmicks – many of the tricks in this book – to turn that class around. I knew I'd succeeded when I was teaching one child chess during a wet break time. A few others were watching, so he taught them how to play. Surprisingly, chess went viral in Year 5. At break time, I had pupils asking to take chess boards outside so they could play in the sun! Many of those taking part had previously caused problems during free time, and now they were obviously behaving differently.

At the front of the class, we had a Velcro strip onto which we had stuck everybody's names. They started in random locations. The rule was that if they beat somebody, they swapped places. The bottom ten names were all in a random circle so that there was no 'bottom place'. The funniest moment was when someone in that circle beat the number one and swapped with them. The chess league was enjoyed by everyone and completely managed by the children.

PROTECT YOUR WHITEBOARD PENS

Always keep your whiteboard pens in a nice location near your board. Even better, get some Velcro – stick some to your whiteboard, and the other side around your pen. That way you'll always know where your pens are. The same works for your board rubber.

Be warned, so will everybody else! So always keep a spare set somewhere clearly visible – they don't have to be new. If everybody knows where the spare set is too, they'll go for those instead of going for the ones near your board.

Finally, keep your actual backup spare set somewhere safe and slightly tricky to get to – like the back of your desk drawer. That way you'll know that you can find a working pen when you need it.

ONLY PUT THE DATE ON THE BOARD ON MONDAY

I was rubbish at remembering to change the date. My Year 3 class used to tell me off all the time. And then they began to autocorrect! One day, they just gave up on my ability to tell them the date and started to work it out.

Obviously, when a new month starts, you might want to change the date, and I always updated the date on Monday mornings, but otherwise they would work it out themselves. One less job for you to worry about!

BORROWING PENCILS/EQUIPMENT

Too many times I've observed teachers in classrooms and a child has put their hand up to say they don't have a pencil or something to write with. Momentarily flustered, the teacher then scrambles around only to find that all the spares have already been given out and lost.

This is easily remedied.

Every time somebody borrows something from you, write their name on the board. Their name is only removed when they return the item into your hands. This last part is important – you don't want random pencils on your desk, or a loophole where someone keeps something but claims it is returned. And don't let them leave the class until they have returned whatever they have borrowed.

If the same name keeps appearing, you could try giving them

something permanently, but if they just lose it anyway, better to use the list system as it will teach them responsibility. And that is the real end goal, after all.

BORROWING PENCILS FOR PERIPATETIC TEACHERS

This is a bonus top tip really designed for those teachers that go from class to class. There is nothing worse than turning up in somebody else's classroom and finding children don't have the basic tools they need to complete your lesson, especially when you can't find where the teacher in charge of that room has hidden their stash of spare resources.

At one point in my career, I was an MFL teacher, delivering French to every child in the school for 40 minutes each week. I carried with me a pot of pencils. As each child entered the class, I would hand them a pencil. They were not allowed to leave until they had handed a pencil back to me. I will be honest – by the end of the year I had quite a collection of pencils, and they were very rarely the ones I had started with!!! In some years, I even managed to finish with MORE pencils.

But this did teach each class to be responsible and did ensure that missing equipment didn't slow down my lessons.

HAVE A TOILET BOOK

At one point I grew concerned about the number of pupils leaving to use the bathroom. I started writing down their names in a book. I did absolutely nothing with that information. But the idea that their trip was recorded was a nudge that made them less likely to go.

Children who have a medical need to use the bathroom regularly were treated differently. In every single case, I had a conversation with them, and we agreed that I would still write their name down, but they were aware it was just to make sure they were okay and that there wouldn't be any repercussions. I explained to one concerned parent that by writing down when their child had used the toilet, I was also able to create a detailed picture of how it was affecting her education, which resulted in their GP speeding up the support process. Data really is everything!

DON'T DISPLAY THE DAILY TIMETABLE

This is a habit that needs to stop. It wastes teachers' time and doesn't help children at all.

I was told by multiple educational psychologists that having a timetable was vital for pupils with special needs. They were wrong. Having a timetable THAT DIDN'T CHANGE was helpful, but if you've been in a classroom for more than a week, you know that your plans constantly change.

Instead, I would talk through what they could expect, along with possible changes. Any changes to the school day were discussed with the class as soon as I knew. The class all trusted that if anything different was coming up, they would be told. At one point my class contained 5 different autistic children – every single one trusted me completely and when they moved to their next class said that the classroom timetable had begun to stress them out again, because every time they looked at it, they were worried that it might change.

Let's remove this time-wasting habit and start talking to our classes. Let's be teachers that provide safety and reassurance that, no matter what happens, we will make sure the day runs as smoothly as possible for this in our care.

I heard a phrase recently that sums up my feelings about being a TA, and that is 'every interaction is an intervention' – I don't know who coined it. So, I would say, seek to make a connection by listening to a child and responding appropriately so they understand they are valued for who they are, not for what they can or can't do. In terms of top tip for an intervention, I would say, know when to stop! Just because you have a time slot allocated, doesn't mean you've got to use it all. Stop while the child/group are still enjoying the activity and before they start to flag or lose interest.

Becky Bale

3

Displays

Displays are incredibly personal. They will help identify your class as your own, so for many of these tips I talk about things I used to do. I wouldn't recommend that you follow all of this advice, but you might spot something that inspires you to be creative in your classroom. Embrace creativity and make it so that when people enter the room, they know it's yours.

SORT OUT YOUR COLOURED DRAWING PINS

Okay, you may think I go too far with this one but trust me. Visual stress is a real thing, and many classrooms are overloaded with colour to the point that pupils stop taking notice and feel on edge the whole time. To reduce visual stress, I organised all my colourful drawing pins into plastic cups according to their colour (or you could ask some sensible volunteers to do it for you). Then, whenever I put posters up on the wall, the colour of the pin matched the colour of the corner of the poster.

I still remember teachers coming into my class for a training evening – one noticed that all the 'red hat questions' had red pins. They paused for a moment to ponder my insanity then said, "That's just so satisfying".

It may be a little thing, but it made a huge difference.

Again, in case you're worried about my obsessive attention to detail, I also used to store the drawing pins in separate plastic cups according to colour. The cups stacked perfectly, meaning I could easily get to the right colour and store my manic compulsion neatly.

CREATE CHRISTMAS ARTWORK

I love Christmas in Primary School. Too much, if that's possible. Children get so excited, and the opportunity for going all out is far too easy. One of my favourite activities was to take a digital photo of each person in the class – get them to take them if possible.

We then opened copies of those pictures in art editing software such as Paint.NET[2]. They were tasked with doodling on their faces to add a Christmas theme. The only rule was that I had to still be able to recognise it was them – no completely covered faces. Some children drew the most incredibly detailed snowflakes falling from the sky. Some gained antlers and red

2   https://www.getpaint.net

noses. Many had beards and red hats. The great part was printing them off and putting every single one on display. Despite covering digital art and improving mouse control and dexterity, the children just saw it as Christmas fun. They absolutely adored the gallery that was formed as they realised what different people had digitally doodled.

ALWAYS USE PASTEL BACKING PAPER

This is another one that you may think is crazy but trust me – it works! The first thing I did in any new classroom was tear down any backing paper that wasn't sky blue or green. I wanted my room to be filled with natural colours – not dark purples and bright reds. Children may be attracted to bright things, but so are moths and it doesn't do them any good. Calm colours allow them to see what's on the display – which is the whole point of having a display – and changes the atmosphere of the room.

As a teacher, I have always been someone that other staff come to when they need to offload their stress. At first, people would just approach me wherever I was and ask for a chat, which I was more than happy to do. But then I noticed a shift – they started to ask if we could talk "in my room". I decided to ask a couple of people why – it might have been something to do with confidentiality or privacy – but was surprised by their answer. "Your room is just so calming."

My choice of calming colours wasn't just affecting the children – it was affecting the staff too!

FIRST DISPLAY

Most teachers get an opportunity to meet their new classes in July before they officially start in September. I always made a point of asking every child to draw a rough self-portrait, write a sentence or two about themselves, and add some keywords or drawings (depending on their age) linked to their character. I would then cut these out into paint splat shapes, back them on further paint splats and make a display so that when they entered my class, they could already see their work. This gave them ownership of the class from day one – it wasn't a room that they were ABOUT to put their stamp on; it was already theirs.

This helped remove anxiety early on, but also helped set the tone. This class was going to be their home for the next year and they were going to be responsible for looking after and decorating it.

And why paint splats? Because when you walk into a classroom at the start of term that is perfectly tidy and organised it can be quite daunting. Initially, the children joining me were also new to the school as I worked in a Juniors-only school. I wanted them to know that it was going to be a creative classroom.

CREATE A VICTORIAN BLACKBOARD

I know I said always use pastels, but for the Victorian topic I would turn the main display black. I also had a very artistic teaching assistant who wrote the word 'Victorian' in beautiful chalk writing. I would annotate the display in chalk, drawing frames around posters. I also used brown border paper to simulate the wooden frame.

I hated how dark and dominating it was, but it proved how much the atmosphere can change just through a choice of colours.

EMBRACE THE ADVENTURE

During a space topic, I realised that my class all loved *Doctor Who*. So, I used blue sugar paper with white blocks to recreate the TARDIS door on the classroom front door. They definitely entered the room with a greater sense of anticipation that learning would be an adventure that could take them anywhere! When the topic ended, the TARDIS door remained.

POSE QUESTIONS

There was a fad a while back about creating visually powerful interactive displays. Belair[3] has published an amazing series packed full of ideas.

But one really simple way of making displays interactive and useful is by covering them in questions that you've already answered. As children glance up, they'll be reminded of the answer. It's also possible to fold a piece of paper in half, putting the question on the outside and the answer on the inside. If children forget the answer, they can lift the flap to find out more.

The best way to start this sort of thing is to have some jokes or riddles. This will get the children used to seeing engagement as a fun thing. Then transfer the same concept to science or topic work and you'll be surprised at how many children continue to engage.

KEEP THE BACKING PAPER

You've probably already worked out that I like to be incredibly organised, and I like to save time. Well, this stretches to the backing paper too! At the end of a unit, I carefully remove the display AND carefully remove the backing paper. I roll it up and save it for next year. After all, it is already cut to size and is probably good for at least three years. It's easily stored

3   https://www.redboxbooks.co.uk/publishers/collins-education/belair-on-display/

and means you can quickly recreate the display from the previous year.

GET FREE CHRISTMAS DECORATIONS

I love Christmas, but when I was given my first classroom I had no decorations for my class. Rather than spend money on new decorations, I went onto various FreeCycle[4] websites and social media discussion groups. I ended up getting a small Christmas tree and a box of decorations from a newly retired teacher, as well as lots of other bits and pieces that helped make the classroom look amazing. All for nothing.

CHRISTMAS PLAN 1

From the 1st of December, begin to make your class a Christmas grotto. Each day add something different. In my first class, this is exactly what I did, and the class loved coming in and discovering new things. Some teachers worried that the children would become over-excited by the end of term. In fact, the opposite was true. They had time to burn out some of their Christmas excitement as it had continued for so long. They also got rid of some of their energy by searching for each day's new thing.

---

4   https://www.freecycle.org

CHRISTMAS PLAN 2

One year, for some reason, I did things differently. I had a particularly energetic class and I knew that searching for something every single day would cause problems. I needed them to be bored of Christmas before it came. So, on the last day of November, I stayed late at work and completely decorated my classroom. Check the list below for a few of the things I used to do. The class was over excited on the first day, but within a week 'Christmas' was normal.

1. Full-size Christmas tree in the corner
2. Half-size Christmas tree in the sink
3. 3D corrugated cardboard fireplace in front of the radiator (so that it felt warm)
4. Cuddly toys by the fireplace to look cute
5. Decorations hanging from the ceiling
6. Santa's suit hung up on the back of the door
7. Digital photos of every child that they'd doodled on to look Christmassy
8. Table centrepieces
9. Snow effect display paper (available in various school supplies catalogues)
10. A life-size cuddly penguin sat in the corner
11. Various penguin models were scattered throughout the class (I liked penguins)
12. A sign saying Merry Christmas was on the window –

two-sided so it could be read on both sides

13. Fairy lights around the whiteboard

14. A nativity display (the best one we created was silhouettes – very artistic)

15. A small Christmas tree on top of the filing cabinet, surrounded by cubes the children had decorated with pictures of their strengths – I pointed out afterwards that these were gifts

16. And lots of small little touches throughout the displays – like penguins poking their heads around the corner of posters, or a giant Christmas pencil somebody had given me resting on my desk

My very artistic teaching assistant painted me the most enormous, life-like copies of the Gruffalo and various characters from the books using poster paint. You would have thought they were photocopies from the books! She ended up leaving the school to launch her own business creating posh teddy bears. Always make the most of the skills that your team might have! You're not taking advantage – you're celebrating their contribution. Remember to be grateful!

SAVE DISPLAY MATERIALS

Save everything. It'll save work in future years. Save all display materials – I've already mentioned I even saved the backing paper to save time. In one school I used a drawer for each term, in another I had a folded piece of sugar paper and inserted the correct resources inside. The following year, I could just pull out the ready-made resources. It saved me days and days!

Even better, it meant that when I prepared a resource, I could put a little more time into it, knowing it would be saved and filed ready for next year.

I would keep props stored in a similar way – blue glass balls that looked good on the Antarctic display, or the bird-shaped kite that flew from the projector during our rainforest topic – were kept in drawers/boxes clearly labelled with the term.

I also kept writing templates that had been filled in, or examples of text from Literacy Working Walls. These would provide inspiration for the following year as instead of starting from the beginning again, I could build on and improve what I'd taught previously.

CREATE MORE EXCITING CLASSROOMS

Your classroom is an opportunity for adventure. Make it look exciting. If you're not already inspired, here are a few more ideas:

India – we draped saris from the projector in the centre of the class to the edges to create a tent effect. It cools the classroom nicely if done during the hot summer months.

The Rainforest – we had ivy draped on a suspended string, and a large bird kite hanging from the ceiling (both sourced from car boot sales). My poor teaching assistant also cut out many, many hand-sized black ants. At the start of the unit, there were a few crawling out from an ant hole. By the end of term, the stream of ants went around the entire classroom.

Bridges – we cut out a giant bridge to go over the windows

Space – we took photos of every child in the class pretending to hold a lightsaber then used an app to edit in that magical object. The class Jedi army was born.

Ancient Greece – we created a Greek temple, surrounding it with the fake ivy from the rainforest display. Making pillars from rolled-up card worked much better than we'd anticipated!

Antarctica – we created an igloo out of old plastic milk cartons and used it as a reading corner. We also covered everything with fake snow fabric.

You'll notice they all start 'we'. Class displays were very much a team effort as my artistic skills were lacking, even if my vision was ambitious. I could not have achieved anything without the help of my amazing teaching assistants!

See the Belair on Display[5] book series for more incredible, inspirational ideas. And remember, keep your display materials for future years.

5   https://www.redboxbooks.co.uk/publishers/collins-education/belair-on-display/

4

Behaviour Management

ALLOW FIDDLE TOYS

You've probably seen plenty of fiddle toys for children who need something to distract themselves or redirect their energy. However, the best fiddle toy I've ever found is a Rubik's Cube. This intelligent toy not only has a great feel for the fidgeting child but there is also a sense of purpose. Teaching children to channel their fidgets into something with purpose is a great way of ensuring they learn that their energy doesn't have to be wasted.

SAY THANK YOU TO GET WHAT YOU WANT

"Thank you for writing your name, Noah" or "I'm so pleased you're focusing on your work" – that second one is spoken in the present tense. It presumes that the pupil is already going to follow your instruction. Instead of telling somebody off for not focusing, you're praising them for following your prompt.

CASE STUDY

There was a child in my class who had been described as lazy by every teacher he had ever had. It turned out that the pace of lessons was too slow for him and he just needed his mind occupying while he waited for everybody to catch up. I gave him a Rubik's Cube and asked him to try and solve it. After a while, I sat and taught him how to do the first few steps – there are plenty of instructions online that help with this. Within a few weeks, he was teaching other children how to solve their own cubes until my modern classroom looked like it had been hit an 80's revival. The class all loved being able to show off their new skill to friends and family alike. The best part of all? Everyone was learning how to follow long sequences of instructions, which was having a positive impact on their ability to follow instructions in the class.

DON'T SPLIT UP CHILDREN THAT DISTRACT EACH OTHER

Teach children how to work together rather than moving them around – worth it in the long run. Remember you are creating a class community, not just managing education. If they learn to work with people, then those skills will pass on when they leave school. People used to like receiving my class because they all got on with each other. And before you presume that my kids started off perfectly behaved, I was always given the 'characters'!

CASE STUDY

One parent had emailed me. The other was at my classroom door first thing in the morning. Both were unhappy and wanted their children separated. Apparently, both children had said that they weren't able to work because they were distracted. I asked both parents if this was a long-term issue. They said yes. I asked what strategies previous teachers had used. They told me they'd been sitting apart every time. I asked if they wanted it sorted for good. They said yes. I told them their children would stay sitting next to each other.

I then spent the next few weeks focusing on teaching both children how to manage their distractions. As they spent all their lessons together, with no imminent prospect of being split up, they began to play with other people during break times. There were no furtive glances across the class causing problems. They were set quantity targets for their work. Initially, these were easily achievable, so they believed they were working at their full capacity (they weren't). Gradually these were increased until they were more realistic.

It took time, but both pairs of parents, at their final Parents Evening with me, thanked me for investing the time and energy in sorting out their children's problems. Over the next three years of primary school, the problem never resurfaced again.

The lesson? Don't take the easy route of splitting up children.

Instead, work out what is causing the problem and deal with it. Long term, it's worth it! Case Study Note

I need to add a proviso to this. I've always had classes that were full of characters. And my Autumn term data was always a little lacking. Data analysts don't like that. By the end of the year, my data always beat expectations, despite me not exactly following the rules. It was because I had invested in the social aspects of my class so that there were fewer distractions later on in the year.

I will admit, there were children who I did need to separate at times. Sometimes they needed to be apart before they could learn to work together. You'll need to use your judgement. But the key tip here is NEVER separate children without ALSO working to solve whatever was causing the distraction. Separating children doesn't solve anything long term.

EXPECT CALM

My classroom has always been an oasis of calm. Even in noisy lessons where lots of things are going on, there is a calmness to the apparent chaos. That's because I have very clear expectations.

Just to be clear, I have set these expectations with every class I've ever had, including when I've been a supply teacher. And I've achieved my goal every time.

First, if people come into your class noisy, send them out. Start again. Congratulate the quiet ones. Give them your attention. Thank them for listening. Also, thank the noisier ones who are suddenly quiet – reward their behaviour change.

Second, maintain the expectation. Make a point of having silence at some point, so that when the silence begins to break, you can re-establish that silence with a phrase like "2 more minutes of silence before we start talking, thank you...". This extends their 'silent working' perseverance subtly.

Third, don't raise your voice. Ever. Use some of the strategies littered throughout this book to manage behaviour silently and quietly. If you are allowed to raise your voice, so are they. Model the expectation.

On that last point, it's also worth explaining when a loud voice is allowed. For example, in an emergency you might say 'stop'. But never raise your voice when you're angry – go quiet instead. It's much, much more effective.

THREE STRIKES AND YOU'RE OUT

In my first-ever full-time class, I encountered a child who would not stop shouting out. It was as though he was unaware of the world around him. Looking back, he was probably autistic and I didn't have enough experience at the time to realise it. I do remember talking to the Special Needs Co-ordinator and asking for help.

She turned to me and gave me the best top tip I have ever received.

Give him permission to shout out three times, but no more.

At first, he had 'three strikes' per lesson. After a while, I realised he wasn't using them up until the end of the morning, and then it lasted the whole day.

Instead of asking the impossible – no more shouting out – I'd given him a target to improve. He had achieved that target in small steps and, eventually, he stopped shouting out. This was a long process, but I got where I wanted to get by starting with a small step.

BEHAVIOUR CHARTS AND DETENTIONS ARE OPPORTUNITIES FOR DISCUSSION

It is one thing to give somebody detention, a punishment or a sad face on a behaviour chart. It is another to sit with them and discuss what went wrong. It is even better to discuss the strategies that can be used to avoid that behaviour in the first place.

PROVIDE CLEAR INSTRUCTIONS

Make sure your intonation matches your intention. It's possible to say stop in such a way that the entire class freezes. Or to say it in such a way that the entire class thinks you're asking

CASE STUDY

At my first school, we had a traffic light behaviour system. Any child who misbehaved risked being moved from green to amber. Repeated bad behaviour during the week might lead to red, or to 'special measures.' Amber or red would mean missing part of Golden Time – the weekly 30 minutes of free play every child enjoyed inside the classroom.

This was the time that those children who would normally be sat outside got special attention from me. We would discuss what went wrong, why it had happened and how to prevent it from happening again. The rewards in my class were never for perfect behaviour – they were for improved behaviour and then for consistently improved behaviour. We started where we were, rather than aspiring for perfection. By focusing on improvement, things became manageable.

a question. It's important to get this right. In an emergency, you need to class to recognise your urgent tone of voice and follow your instructions. They need to trust the strength of your voice. Speak with absolute authority. Short sentences. Clear instructions.

I used to find saying the word 'And' before I started to speak was really useful in getting people's attention. 'Annnnnnd Stop.' The class would begin to listen so that they knew what the instruction was. This simple audio cue vastly improves the obedience success rate.

CASE STUDY

There was one girl in my class that I had taught in year 3 and year 5. At age 7 she had been the model pupil; she was everything a teacher would want. In year 4, she mixed with the wrong children and by year 5 she had become a distraction. However, it quickly became clear that she was better behaved than most but didn't know how to hide it as well. I used her as a warning light. If she needed to be told off, it meant others had needed to be told off for some time! During our 'golden time' punishment talks, I would teach her the strategies that the others had mastered long ago. I taught her how to hide misbehaviour. Why? Because she was becoming disillusioned. She knew the others were worse than her but couldn't work out why they weren't being caught. By the end of the year, she was no longer standing out as a naughty child. In fact, she had begun to feel like she could trust adults again and was no longer disillusioned.

YOUR NAME IS POWER

This one may be more for supply teachers, but it's worth sharing here. When I've covered classes in schools that don't know who I am, I am very careful to set the tone from the start. I start by barely speaking to the class as they enter – I want them to recognise I'm watching. I might put my finger to my lips and signal that they need to sit down but very little else. During the register, I often drop in a joke at the end, saying it'll be hard to remember their names, so they're all called Bob from now on. I then point out that they've been so well behaved I started to relax and become funny. But the most important part of my supply arsenal – whether it be in primary or secondary classrooms – is that I never share my name. I am 'Sir' – I remain an unknown quantity for as long as possible. With one class, I remember starting to write my name on the board during a lesson, then stopping halfway through. I kept the tension going.

I appreciate this seems counter-intuitive. You want the class to warm to you so that all anxieties are removed. However, I have found – including working with special needs pupils – that what they want from any teacher is authority. They need someone who will maintain order and set clear boundaries so that they can relax, knowing where they stand. By attempting to come across as a friendly person, it is harder to make those boundaries clear. But by starting hard, then relaxing quickly, then returning to hard again, they understand your expectations, but also appreciate that there is the potential for you to be the perfect supply teacher.

GET THE CLASS SILENT WHEN YOU WANT THEM SILENT

When counting down from 5 to 1, use your fingers as a visual prompt. Those children that instantly stop then have something to look at.

I used to use my fingers, and for the 1, move my finger to my lips to demonstrate silence. I'd then nod and smile at those people who also had their finger on their lips and were ready to listen. The class would soon be silent.

That said, if you've got that one person who isn't silent, you could always start writing their name slowly on the board. Someone will quickly nudge them. If you finish writing their name, you could add some consequences.

Not saying their name has extra power and means that you're also following the expectation that the class will be silent. The next noise you make will be positive and productive, and your actual interaction with that noisy child when they do stop is positive as you haven't actually said their name.

There was one occasion when a student teacher asked me how I got the class silent. I stood up. The class went silent. I explained that it had taken a lot of training, reminding them of expectations. Be consistent and you will achieve success.

HAVE CONSEQUENCES NOT PUNISHMENTS

Children all recognise punishments. They don't always see them as fair, but they recognise them!

What they need to understand are the consequences. They need to understand that they have responsibility for how they engage with and enjoy the school experience, and that when they put in the effort they will be rewarded. But each person's effort begins at a different level. For some, simply sitting still will have been a huge effort that only meets your 'basic' expectations and therefore receives no reward.

For all forms of punishment or expectation, explain clearly what you want and keep to what you've said. Any consequence that doesn't actually happen (whether it be positive or negative) will result in a disheartened response from the pupil. The way you keep your word will also change how much your class trusts you.

In computing terms, we could say: IF you do this, THEN this will happen. Make it clear that they are making a choice. Add in an extra layer of reward: IF you do this, THEN you will be rewarded, ELSE you will be punished.

A word of warning with this strategy. PLEASE do not set your children up to fail. This is not a way to make them responsible for their punishment. This is a way to give them responsibility for making steps in the right direction AWAY from punishment. Consider offering them chances (see the 'three strikes' top tip) or discussing strategies with them to help achieve the reward. Show that you're on their side, wanting them to win.

WRITE THE NUMBER 30 ON THE BOARD

This is my favourite behaviour management strategy. When a

class is being noisy, or you want their attention and they haven't responded to other strategies, silently walk to the whiteboard and start to draw the number 30 as slowly as possible. If you manage to finish drawing the number, they lose 30 seconds of their playtime. If (heavens forbid) you finish the 30 and they're still talking, just write a plus followed by another 30!

I'll admit that when I'm in a bad mood and feeling impatient, I might write just a little faster to ensure the class misses their break time.

You'll find that the quiet, attentive children soon encourage everyone else to be quiet because they don't want to lose their break when they've behaved. Generally speaking, I'll do this with my back to the class, but my TA sometimes mentioned children that had been silent the whole time and I'd let them out first when the 30 seconds was up in recognition of their good behaviour.

I've also adapted this for year groups in the past, saying things like "as you're in Year 5 now, it's 50 seconds."

The very first time I do this, I don't warn them what I'm doing either. I'll stand at the board with one finger on my lips and stare occasionally at the clock. At the end, I'll explain what was going on without mentioning their behaviour:

"If I'd finished writing the number 30, you would have lost

30 seconds of your break time. I'm so pleased you're all looking this way now..."

USE ECHOES AND RHYMES

Use class chants to get attention – think about the latest trends, but there are a few that worked for me. Some are timeless, others very much a trend at the time:

1. Ready to make your move ... chihuahua (it's based on an old 90's dance track)
2. Oh no, oh no... oh no no no no no (TikTok)
3. To infinity... and beyond (*Toy Story*)
4. Class 3G ... ready to learn (to the tune of BBC... Radio Two)
5. Hi Ho, Hi Ho... it's off to work we go (classic *Snow White and the Seven Dwarfs* from Disney)

Get the idea? Literally anything can work, and the internet is full of good rhymes and echoes. Make something that's just for your class and embrace it. You'll find your class is united because they have an 'in thing' that they know and nobody else does.

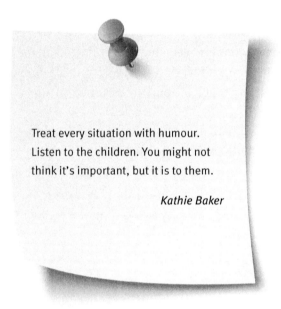

Treat every situation with humour. Listen to the children. You might not think it's important, but it is to them.

Kathie Baker

5

English

SPELLING LISTS ARE A WASTE OF TIME

Children are brilliant at learning something as a one-off, performing well, then forgetting again and making the same old mistakes. Spellings are a great example.

The reality is that spelling lists are simply a way of making parents feel good and giving them a measure of their child's memory skills. Children's spellings began to improve much faster when I abandoned set spelling lists and introduced personalised lists. Each week, children would learn a spelling rule off by heart, along with three keywords that they spelt wrong in their work. The keywords would only ever link to previous spelling rules – that way they were reminded of whatever rule they had forgotten.

How did I manage this? Children are really good at testing each other – we did tests on whiteboards while I walked around. I would do random spot checks on particular children to make sure they'd actually learnt them. I set the culture where children knew that they were working to improve their own spellings, and that taking shortcuts now would only lead to more work later on.

This approach saw a genuine increase in spelling ability in the class, even though parents felt less engaged in the process. To fix this, they were asked to focus on learning multiplication tables, forwards, backwards and out of order. This skill is just as important, but much more appropriate for the rote learning methods usually employed by parents, and also just as suitable to be tested in a rote learning way.

LEARN SPELLINGS IN CURSIVE – THE MUSCLE WILL REMEMBER THE JOINS

I've noticed that sometimes words are harder to spell when I'm typing them. They're definitely harder to spell when I'm sounding them out to somebody! This is because a lot of words are written on automatic pilot. I've handwritten the words "great work" so many times that I can write them neatly, blindfolded, with both hands tied behind my back.

Encourage children to learn their spellings in cursive writing, and they'll soon spell them correctly more consistently.

However, the same is true for the reverse. If you spot a word that is consistently misspelt, then you've got to undo that mental programming. This may involve repeatedly re-writing that word several times every time it is incorrect so that the brain is gradually reprogrammed.

More than this though, repeat the practice at other random times. Don't let that person forget they're focusing on getting that word correct. Make it fun throughout the day to suddenly challenge them to write it correctly on their whiteboard.

HANDWRITING – EVERYTHING YOU NEED TO KNOW

Make a list of the children in your class who do not have good handwriting. And now identify why...

1. Is it because they are unable to hold a pen properly? Maybe their hand isn't strong enough to push down on a pencil and a pen would actually be easier! Maybe a pen grip would make all the difference in the world. Give them a tennis ball or sponge ball and ask them to squeeze it to exercise and build their muscles.

2. Maybe they do not have good coordination skills – draw some circles and ask them to go from touching their nose to touching the centre of each circle as fast as they can. How accurate are they? Invest in a handwriting doodle book – *Write from the Start* by Ion Teodorescu[6] is a great resource!

6   https://www.amazon.co.uk/Write-start-Perceptual-Handwriting-Teodorescu/dp/B00CB5YQFM/

3. Maybe there is a barrier bigger than you understand and can fix by asking that child to write lines over and over.

Have a conversation with the parents and ask them to try the following:

1. Big chalk writing – cover the pavement with one letter drawn perfectly
2. Water pistol – squirt the same letter over and over again onto a wall or garage door
3. Finger painting – actually sticking your finger in paint and making pictures of various words
4. Painting with a fine brush – it'll be messy and look bad, but the hand is making the right movements

Both of these will help develop muscle memory, and they're fun activities that parents can do with their child. Definitely more interesting than writing the same thing over and over.

There may be situations where there is a medical reason for a child's poor handwriting. The process for discovering this is relatively easy too. The parent simply has to approach their GP and ask for an Occupational Therapy referral. Sometimes, children are given recommendations for slopes to write on, or pen grips, or even squeezing balls to increase finger muscle strength. But there were two particularly interesting discoveries.

CASE STUDY

In my first class was a child who had some of the most illegible handwriting I'd ever seen. He was also clumsy, often bumping into things, and had a strong dislike of sports lessons. After consulting with our Special Needs Co-ordinator, I agreed to speak with the parents about a referral.

When she came back from the Occupational Therapist, she was incredibly grateful. It turned out her son had a muscular weakness that meant he was physically unable to write effectively. *(Note, I don't blame his previous teachers – he never mentioned the pain, not even to his parents.)*

Now he was entitled to a computer and everything he did was typed. It made a huge difference and his progress skyrocketed.

HIDE STORIES IN ENVELOPES

Shared writing has come a long way over the past couple of decades. Writing a paragraph of text with a whole class is still a really important activity, demonstrating and modelling how to write effectively. One of my favourite things to do is have a pre-written sample text hidden in two locations – one near me where I can see it and nobody else can, and another in an envelope at the back of the class.

I carefully guide the class, gently nudging their ideas and leading them towards my example text. Once it's written, I

CASE STUDY

I had been given an interesting class that included one person with appalling handwriting who was clearly intelligent. I was told "he's probably dyslexic, but we don't diagnose that so just keep on him." I decided to watch him closely and investigate further. I discovered a very bright boy with a great sense of humour. He was also incredibly bendy and loved showing off how flexible he was. I cannot eat gluten, and he shared that he had acid reflux issues so also avoided gluten.

At the first Parents Evening, I asked whether this 10-year-old had ever been referred to an Occupational Therapist for his handwriting. I was told no. I was told that his handwriting had been a constant complaint – every target ever set had been handwriting – and nothing that they did made any difference. I asked her to have her son referred.

A short while later, the mum made a point of visiting me. I still remember it vividly. She was so grateful. It turns out her son had a muscular condition that affected everything, including his stomach muscle! Doctors had started him on medication, told him to stop overstretching his joints, and were now prepared for what was to come. Apparently, his teenage years could have been much worse without the knowledge of his condition.

What triggered this discovery? His poor handwriting.

My decision to act made a difference to that child that will last for the rest of his life. Never forget the potential impact you have on every child you teach.

ask someone sensible to stand up, which they do nervously. I ask them to go to the back of the class and fetch the sealed envelope. I then ask them to read it out loud.

The reaction from the class the first time I do this is one of wonder and awe. They genuinely believe they came up with the ideas themselves. The extra emotional hit from this event helped them all remember the sentence structures we'd introduced. It's not a trick I can do every time or even more than once with each class, but certainly something worth trying!

LEARN A POEM

There is something special about performing together as a class, so during the very first week of any school year I would teach everybody the same poem – *Hand on the Bridge* by Michael Rosen[7]. We would learn actions, improve our performance and then go outside at the end of the day and perform it to parents. I always made sure I videoed the 'show' for those parents that wouldn't get to see their child shine.

This helped the class gain cohesion very early on. We were all working together for a common goal. Often the performance part was 'spontaneous' – in other words, I didn't tell the children we might actually perform until 5 minutes before

7   https://www.youtube.com/watch?v=N4sCaAFkcwI

the end of a school day. I'd say something like… "Ooh, you're all really good at that poem; wouldn't it be great if we performed it to all the parents outside waiting to collect you…"

It boosted the class AND it boosted my own reputation. It was a very public display that we were a class community.

RETIRED PEOPLE LOVE TO HEAR CHILDREN READ

I once contacted several local churches hunting for retired people who would be willing to work with a year group that had particularly low reading skills. My mission was simple – I wanted as many children as possible to be heard reading every single day. The elderly didn't disappoint. We gave them training in how to sound out words, how to be positive, and permitted them to award team points. We also encouraged them to "do the voices", which children absolutely loved! There were some real characters among my Elderly Army that truly inspired that year group and had an incredible impact on their love of reading.

6

Maths

CALCULATORS ARE YOUR FRIEND

There is a lie told to children that the best way to do maths is in your head; that calculators are the last resort. The reality is that, thanks to mobile phones, children will have calculators on them at all times. Worse still, they won't use them as calculators. In supermarkets, they won't compare prices accurately, relying instead on 'head maths' and guesses. They won't compare prices online effectively. They will lose out because we encourage them to avoid calculators rather than embracing the usefulness of technology at our disposal.

Remember, the 2010 National Curriculum permits you to go above and beyond the curriculum (and also claims that there is time in the school day to do this – let's not go there). I would like to suggest that learning how to do practical maths, including using a calculator in real-life situations, is essential. Children need to see that they can harness technology to their benefit; it is not a cheat!

One way to engage children with calculators easily is to create a 'Checker Station' in your classroom. Once they have completed a series of questions, they can visit the station, use a calculator, and see if they get the same answer. If the answers don't match, they have to decide: did I use the calculator in the wrong way, or did I make a mistake? Note that I'm not asking them to believe the calculator is always right – I'm asking them to evaluate both their mental maths and calculator skills. This is especially important with BIDMAS/BODMAS style questions, where the order they complete calculations can alter the answer.

NUMBER LINES ARE YOUR FRIEND

One of the most exciting things I have ever discovered in maths is that number lines are incredibly useful for explaining what is going on in my head. In fact, they become even more useful for calculating addition and subtraction of time, because I choose the jump sizes and don't get confused by the whole '60 minutes' maths that fools so many.

Even at GCSE maths, I encourage pupils to demonstrate their thinking using written methods and jottings. The most effective way is the number line. Often, children tell me that I've drawn what is happening in their head. But in their head, they made a mistake because they couldn't hold all the information.

The number line is a vital tool that provides a way of children doing quick mental maths with the help of appropriate jotting. They can literally see the numbers and what is happening to them, and that picture will eventually become so embedded in their thinking that they use the tool less and less.

LOOK AFTER YOUR CUBES

This may seem a little over the top. Ever had those cubes that stick together? I made sure mine were stored in sticks of 12. That meant that they were easier to hand out during maths lessons, knowing how many sticks each table had. It also routed out the random wrongly shaped cubes that weren't supposed to be there, so they were returned to their true home.

And yes, I did my best to make each stick the same colour.

I know.

Sometimes my level of organisation goes too far.

That said, there's always a child who would benefit from counting sets of numbers, so you've always got a volunteer ready, and you can claim it's for their maths.

Oh, and why 12 and not 10? Easy. 12 has more factors. You can split sticks of 12 into groups of 2, 3, 4 and 6. A stick of 10 can only be split into 2 and 5. Sticks of 12 provide much more flexibility for a variety of maths topics.

HEADS DOWN THUMBS UP – BONUS ENGAGEMENT

I might have adapted the rules to this game a little to make it use up more mental energy. If you don't know the game, the teacher picks four people to stand at the front. Everybody else closes their eyes, puts their heads on the table and sticks up their thumbs. The four volunteers (I might have stuttered the word victim – "victi, er, I mean, volunteers") then have to sneak around the class while the teacher counts down from 10 to 1. They must squeeze one person's thumb, who would then turn their thumb down so that everyone knows they'd been picked. Once the countdown is finished, the people who have been squeezed must guess who squeezed them. If they guess correctly, they replace their 'squeezer'.

I added a couple of small elements to this.

First, I asked people who had been squeezed to stand behind the person they thought had picked them. This meant that I could knock out two or three at a time if they'd all stood behind the same person. It also led to more of a reaction from the rest of the class as they watched what was going on.

Second, I didn't always count from 10 to 1. Sometimes I would count down in 2s, except I would miss out one of the numbers. The class would also have to try and listen for the error and would get bonus points if they could identify where I'd gone wrong.

Third, once a child had taken part – either already squeezed or one of the initial four – they only put one thumb up instead of two. People picking could still choose anyone but were gently encouraged to include anyone that had not been chosen yet. This helped build a greater sense of community in the class.

Finally, if there were only a very small number at the end that had missed out, they would be chosen to be my initial lineup of four people the next time we played.

COUNT DOWN IN LETTERS

It can be really irritating during a maths lesson to count down in numbers, especially when you're rushing to the final answer. So, to avoid silly mistakes, I tend to count down in letters. Yes – when children are working with numbers I count down in letters and when they are working with letters I count down in numbers.

On a personal level, I used to just count down from E. Then I started counting from F. After a few years, I could count down from Z. Being able to say the alphabet backwards is a nice party trick that you can actually learn and rehearse while working.

MINI ME MEASURING

I used to find the measuring activities insanely boring. They were always "measure five items in your class" or "draw five lines in your book." Even the worksheet where you had to give a group of hedgehogs the right length spikes was basically just drawing lines.

Introducing the Mini Me!

Create a small table with two columns: body part and length. Choose your difficulty carefully:

Level 1: Length of arm, length of leg, distance from waist to head, circle around the head

Level 2: Split legs and arms into upper and lower, add feet, add shoulders and waist

Level 3: Add around the wrists, around the forehead instead of the circle, and go from waist to top of the head rather than waist to bottom of the head.

The first thing children do is get a measuring tape and take their partners measurements. You can talk about safe touch if need be (I just told them to be sensible), and make sure they are partnered with the same gender, potentially working in a three. You might also need to remind them that they only need to measure one arm (usually). You can choose how accurate to be – nearest cm, nearest half cm or nearest mm.

Next, depending on the age, they either use a calculator to half the measurements, or do the maths using a formal or informal method. This completes their research.

Finally, prepare many strips of sugar paper about 2/3 cm wide. Children collect a strip and measure as many of their body parts out. They must write their name and the measurement on each one. They may need reminding to make two arms and legs!

Once they had completed all the sections, they brought them to myself or the trained teaching assistant and I stapled them together. Admittedly, this shrunk their measurements a little due to the overlap, but the principle was the same and staples were the fastest, strongest way to make each model.

When you finish the first one, the look on their faces is amazing. They have a perfectly scaled down version of themselves in stickman form. More importantly, they've been measuring, using that information and measuring out, and enjoying every minute.

REMAINDERS ARE FRACTIONS

I've never really liked the idea of remainders in division. I totally understand the idea of 'leftovers' when it comes to counting objects, but mathematically it always felt a little messy. Instead, why not introduce the idea of fractions. If a number is divided by four, and has one left over, it is just as easy to write ¼ as the remainder. In fact, this is a more mathematically accurate result and will help prepare children's understanding of division for Secondary School.

This can still work when counting objects into groups. Let's imagine we're creating groups of 4, and we have three left over. Instead of saying "three remaining" I would say "we only have three out of the four we need," and write it as a fraction. Teaching this 'code' for describing the remainders works regardless of age.

TABLES CHECKERS

I have been consistently shocked by how few people know these tricks to see if a number is a multiple of another number:

2x: The number is even

3x: When you add the digits of the number up, it is a multiple of 3 (for example $17 = 1+7 = 8$ therefore not in the 3 times table)

4x: Half it. If the number is even, it's in the 4s

5x: It must end in 0 or 5.

6x: Digit sum is in the 3s AND the number is even

7x: No easy pattern – see my other top tip

8x: Half it, half it again. If it's even, it's in the 8s.

9x: Digit sum is in the 9s.

10x: Number ends in 0

11x: The numbers are identical (up to 9 x 11). Beyond that, there's a quick trick for some of them – if the 'outer' digits add up to the middle digit, then it is in the 11s, e.g. 165 is in the 11s because 1+5=6.

7 TIMES TABLE TRICK

Prepare to have your mind blown. Draw a 3 x 3 grid.

First, write the following numbers starting on the top right, going from 1 to 9.

7	4	1
8	5	2
9	6	3

Next write the following numbers in front of them. I like to say "0, 1, 2 then 2, 3, 4 then 4, 5, 6" to get the idea that there is repetition at the start of each line.

0	1	2
2	3	4
4	5	6

You will now have the 7x table. That took you seconds.

07	14	21
28	35	42
49	56	63

You can thank me later.

CHRISTMAS PAPER CHAIN TIMES TABLES

My class LOVED this activity. Cut lots of strips of coloured paper ready to make a paper chain. Assign each colour a different number, e.g., blue = 0, green = 3, yellow = 5. You'll need 10 different colours for each possible digit.

Now, ask children to look at the last digit of each of the times tables. For example, the 5 times table always ends in 5 or 0. Children need to make a paper chain that matches the last digits. For the 5s that would go blue, yellow, blue, yellow (if we used my colour examples above).

The children will love making paper chains, which can decorate your class for a celebration or for Christmas. You can then hold up paper chains and ask children to guess which table they come from.

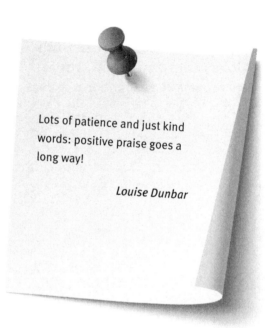

Lots of patience and just kind words: positive praise goes a long way!

Louise Dunbar

7

Assessment

CREATE A CLASS LEARNING JOURNAL

One of the most frustrating, time-wasting things that currently occurs in schools is repetitive evidence collection. During a practical lesson, a photo is taken. That photo is printed thirty times, trimmed and stuck into thirty books. It might then receive a tick from the teacher, or even a generic comment to say that the person engaged in the activity successfully (or not).

At the end of the year, in many schools, those beautifully curated books are then sent home, destroyed or put into cupboards just in case somebody asks to see them. The evidence is 'just in case' but the time it takes to produce is huge.

Here is your solution: Class Learning Journals.

Why not have one book per subject. For example, a class Computing book. In this book, you can stick one copy of the photo under the lesson objective. You might get a couple of children to write what they learned or evaluate some part of the activity. At the end, you can write one teacher comment about learning. Combine this with a record sheet in your assessment file that highlights pupils that struggled and excelled, and your record is complete.

By the end of the year, you'll have a beautiful learning journal for each subject, chronicling the lessons and experiences of your class. And that one book can be treasured or used the following year to see what was taught, what the outcomes were and how to improve lessons for the future.

CREATE A DIGITAL CLASS LEARNING JOURNAL

If you REALLY want to take this to the next level, why not create an online version. Again, it is really tempting to create a learning journal for every child in the class and there are plenty of digital companies offering just such an assessment solution.

My version is a simplified version for the whole class. Create one PowerPoint per subject (other presentation software is available, and Google's auto-saving and backup feature may prove more reliable).

The title for each slide can be the objective. You can insert the picture evidence and get someone in your class to write a couple of sentences about their learning. You could even record their voice or record a short video to insert into the slide.

At the end of the year, this learning journal could then be put online for parents to see or could be distributed via memory sticks or email to parents so that they have a record of their child's learning experiences.

PROVIDE THE ANSWER SHEETS

There is nothing worse than a child completing an hour's worth of maths questions and discovering that every answer is wrong because they've misunderstood something. To avoid this, I provide answer sheets at the start of lessons. They were folded to limit what could be seen, and I never gave out answers for mental maths – only written maths where workings would show whether somebody had copied or not.

I did once catch a child cheating regularly. His autism meant he struggled to understand why he couldn't just look at the answer sheet. It took him longer to see the benefits of being able to check his work, but eventually we got him on-side. Here are a few of the alternative approaches we used to provide answers to the class (and to him in a more secure way):

1. Place answer sheets at the front of the class so children have to walk up to get them
2. Split answer sheets, and place them in different corners of the class to prevent peeking

3. Fold answer sheets so that they gradually unravel to reveal more answer

4. Put answers in envelopes that are held by the teacher and delivered when children are ready – these can also be collected afterwards

5. Include an answer code – each number represents a letter. If the child answers a series of questions correctly, it will spell a word. Note that if they guess the word early, they often cheat for the last couple of letters! It's still quite fun though, and worth doing every now and again.

STAMPS AND STICKERS SAVE SO MUCH TIME

Buy a set of stamps for your teaching assistants to use – "great spelling" or "homework complete". Anything you can do to save time and make things more efficient is worth doing.

Sometimes it's good to consider things in terms of money. For example, how much would it cost to pay a teaching assistant for an hour to complete a task, and how much more could they achieve if they were given better tools.

I also went through a phase of printing off personalised stickers for my class with common complaints (full stops, capitals...) Rather than continually writing the same comments over and over, I'd reach for my trusty stickers.

I also remember creating stickers for the lesson objective. The children left a space on the top corner of the page for the sticker to go. It was much faster than writing it all out and meant they could get straight on with the work.

GROUPING CHILDREN BY COMMON WEAKNESS

We often group children on tables according to their generic ability. But if you have the data from assessments, it's possible to create a temporary seating plan grouping children by their common weaknesses. As you walk around the class, you'll know what one key objective to talk about with each group and it will help keep your conversations focused on the things that will help them the most.

MAIL MERGE PERSONAL TARGETS

Created a worksheet on Word? Do children have personal targets? Create a spreadsheet with those targets on it and then mail merge it onto the worksheet. When the children complete the work, you can also mark it against their personal target without having to refer back to a different document. It's also a very tangible reminder for the children to stay focused on their core target. And as their targets are achieved, you'll have actual evidence in their work, traced through those assessed targets. You'll then be able to set the next target easily by changing the entry in the spreadsheet. All future worksheets will be automatically updated!

MAIL MERGE REPORTS

The mail merge tool will save you hours of writing the same thing over and over. Make sure you put all the information that is common to every child in a spreadsheet – first name, last name, class, teacher name, assessment grades, literacy or numeracy set and relevant teachers (if you use sets). Use the report template provided by your school, and the mail merge tool (Microsoft Word has a clear step by step tool that does most of the work for you).

When you click mail merge, it will automatically put all of that collated data into your reports, saving you hours or repetitive typing.

ASSESSMENT FLAPS

Keeping personal objectives fresh in children's minds can be a challenge. I've seen schools write targets on bookmarks, which usually fall out and get lost. Let's face it, when we read a book, we rarely refer to the bookmark until we've finished!

Instead, open their exercise book to the very last page. Stick a piece of paper into the book so that the edge either sticks out

CASE STUDY

Every single lesson I was infuriated by the work on his page. It was my third teaching practice and this particular Year 3 child lived life in slow motion. The school policy was that the date should be written in full, followed by the full lesson objective, before the actual work could begin. As I glanced back through his book, I took comfort in the fact that his actual class teacher didn't seem to have a solution either.

His book was empty of work.

He was making no progress.

I decided to break school policy and give him permission to work in reverse. Instead of starting with the date and objective, he had to leave a space at the top of his page. His focus was the work, which he began to do. When there were 5 minutes left of the lesson, I would let him know it was time to write the date and title. He would have to finish writing them before he was allowed to go to break.

He was never late going out.

the top or sticks out the side. Use this 'flap' to write or stick their current targets on clearly. Fold the paper so that it is inside the book.

Whenever the children do any work, make sure they unfold their assessment flaps so that they can see their current objective.

You could even ask them to tell the person next to them what their objective is, just so that it is fresh in their mind.

CASE STUDY

I still remember seating a high achieving writer with other people who had failed to use full stops. In an assessment piece she had failed to use them accurately, partially through trying to use punctuation more creatively, but demonstrating a distinct misunderstanding of the role of the full stop.

She was so shocked that she was joining that group, revealing the discriminatory view that she held of her peers. She had ranked herself as better, simply because of her table position. And now she was realising for the first time that everybody was on a personal learning journey, and everybody had their own strengths and weaknesses and could support each other.

Not only did she achieve her goal, but everybody on that table worked together and got on better in the future. There was greater class unity, and a much better understanding of punctuation.

8

Technology

WHITEBOARDS DON'T HAVE TO BE INTERACTIVE

My handwriting isn't great – if I write slowly, everything looks fine, but sometimes I need to pick up the pace to keep the lesson moving and it just looks messy. So, I've used several strategies to overcome my own weaknesses.

First, I made the traditional whiteboard special by putting a colourful border around the edge. This instantly raises the profile of the board. It may only be a small strip of paper, but it makes a huge difference to the way people look at every display in the class.

Second, I used my traditional whiteboard for writing more than my interactive whiteboard. I never use the interactive whiteboard or touchscreen TV unless it actually improves the educational outcomes for my class. Children may focus more initially, but that is because there is change. As a computing specialist, the truth is that computers by themselves don't improve lessons – it's the way you use them and make them special that has the most impact.

USE OF COMPUTER SUITES/LAPTOPS

Take a look at your school's timetable for technology use. You might have a computer suite, or you might have banks of laptops, either of which might be limited in some way. Take a look and see if there is any time when this amazing resource is not being used and could become a regular feature in your own classroom. Remember, technology in itself does not improve outcomes, but the way you use it does.

EVALUATING ACTIVITIES ONLINE

As teachers, we can spend hours trying to find the best online game to support children's learning. However, it is just as easy to give the children the choice. Provide a selection of games and a learning objective and ask the class to try each of the games and work out which one helps them the most. Don't overcomplicate it by adding criteria – the focus isn't really the evaluation, it's the learning. Children will purposefully attempt every activity and find the one that helps them the most.

You might find one activity that everybody hates, in which case you can drop it next year. You might find everyone in agreement, in which case just focus on that one next year. But if you discover disagreement, you've probably got a class with a variety of differing learning styles and you have now successfully adapted to them all by providing a variety of games.

TEACHING PASSWORDS

I once spoke to a teacher about their unit on teaching children to use passwords. They were concerned that after six weeks, their class still couldn't log in. I asked to see their lesson plans. Essentially, these Year 1 children had been asked to log in once at the start of the lesson, then play online games for the rest of the lesson. Teachers would go round and help those that hadn't managed to get in until everyone was playing games.

What a waste of time!

Here's a few quick games that can be played:

1. How many times can you log in and out in 5 minutes
2. Who will log in first (works especially well if the sound is on as it will be the first to play the welcome noise)
3. Pat-a-cake passwords – pat your head after every letter of your password to 'save' it in your memory
4. Handwriting practise using passwords (repetition)
5. Password passes – give out laminated password cards. Reward children who don't need to collect their passes. Make sure the pass has 'Top Secret' at the top.

Also, many network computers need to download the child's profile in order to work. The first time they log on to a computer, it can take longer than usual. I used to pass around a different laptop from the cupboard each day during silent reading. Each child would log in, log out, pass it on. That way, every child had logged onto every laptop at a time when it wasn't urgent.

LEARN TO TYPE

Silent reading happens every single day in many schools. As an adult, I expect you are involved in typing every single day, but rarely have time to read. The reality of the world we live in is that the majority of future employment options will require the ability to type, and efficient typing will do more to boost the economy than learning to read. I'm not dismissing

CASE STUDY

I had just been employed as a class teacher and computing coordinator in a new school and I had just been observed by Senior Leadership for the first time in my new class. In feedback, the Headteacher told me that it was an outstanding lesson, however, he complained saying that he was expecting to see some creative use of technology. I had purposefully chosen not to use any form of technology in that first lesson, so I asked him, "Was the lesson outstanding?" He replied, "Yes."

Technology in itself does not improve outcomes – only the way it is deployed. Children respond to change, so change things up every now and again by teaching an 'old-fashioned' lesson. You'd be surprised just how well they work!

CASE STUDY

I was working with a Year 5 top set that wasn't overly keen on maths. We also used a scheme of work that included a weekly online homework activity that the school wasn't using. I decided to book the computer suite for the last 30 minutes of each Friday's lesson. The entire class would go in as a reward and be able to complete the 'game of the week'. Once complete, they would go on to other suggested online activities, shared through Google Classroom. The great thing was that if an activity wasn't completed, it would remain on their to-do list the following week, allowing me to see which pupils needed more support to get through their list. The computer suite 'reward' actually generated personalised learning for pupils that was incredibly targeted without me needing to do copious amounts of work – a sensible use of technology. Those that finished were encouraged to go onto Times Table Rock Stars. One pupil from that disenfranchised class ended up coming second in a city-wide digital maths tournament.

the importance of reading, but I am suggesting we can upgrade our reading times.

Why not have a computer – it could be a really old one that has been decommissioned as it doesn't need to be on the internet to do this activity – and either run some typing software or give children the opportunity to type up some of their English work. By the end of the year, you would have a whole load of work ready to publish in a memories book without doing any extra work.

Even better, when you do use computers, your class will be much faster at typing and the lesson will be more productive. Their future teachers will thank you too.

USE SHARED DOCUMENTS TO WRITE STORIES

Google Docs allows users to write simultaneously on the same document and see what each person is contributing. This free software is very powerful. Microsoft and others have introduced similar technology to their products.

In Literacy, if you've ever used 'boxed up writing' from the Talk for Writing resources, you'll know that stories are planned in boxes – carefully selected chunks to allow flow from one event to the next. Why not use a shared document so that each member of a table can each contribute their own paragraph – their own box? They can see the edits being made, make collective decisions on changes of direction or the inclusion of key details, and focus on one really good quality paragraph rather than rushing through the whole story.

Or why not put a series of questions, with different children filling in the answers as they find them. Or why not have collaboration between classes or even schools!

There are so many ideas!

RUBBER DUCKS ARE TEACHERS TOO

If you've worked with technology for any length of time, you'll encounter this phenomenon: somebody's computer will fail to behave in the expected way; they will call an expert into the room; they will demonstrate what they did; it will work first time.

So, what happened? When they were trying to complete the task independently, they were in a rush. But when they had to talk through the problem, they slowed down to prove they did everything right. There was no need to call in an expert. They just needed somebody to talk to.

Like a rubber duck.

Every computer needs to have its own rubber duck. Whenever the computer doesn't behave as expected, encourage people to talk to their rubber duck.

I still remember one teacher running into my classroom at lunchtime and saying, "This duck is a genius. I don't know how you do it, but I just talk to him all the time now and my computer works perfectly!"

THEIR PASSWORD IS ALWAYS WORKING!

This is a pet hate. The whole class has tried to log on and one child can't log on properly. They walk up to me and say, "My password isn't working." The truth is that their password IS working, but they are not inputting it correctly. They might be spelling it wrong, using capitals the wrong way or just using completely the wrong word, but the computer is obediently preventing them from entering until they use the correct password.

The computer is doing the right thing.

We must make sure that children do not absolve responsibility for technology failures. We need to teach them that we are the masters – computers work for us, not the other way round. It is not the computer that is at fault – it is the human. We must take responsibility for our actions, not pass the blame to somebody else or (as in this case) an inanimate object.

9

Special Needs

IT'S NOT DYSLEXIA

No teacher likes to admit failure. This is probably why I was told on so many occasions, "We think this one has dyslexia because he definitely doesn't meet our expectations but should." I want to say right now, dyslexia doesn't mean failure. And dyslexia isn't a reason for failure either. What concerned me most about these conversations is that at no point was I told what aspect of their learning was preventing them from making progress.

If you suspect a barrier to learning, investigate. If you can overcome it, your life will be easier. How do you do this? There are several resources online (LUCID COPS[8] is expensive but amazing) and in educational shops that diagnose learning barriers linked to dyslexia. Keep your eyes open for the following:

- Gaps in phonic knowledge
- Visual memory

---

8 https://www.gl-assessment.co.uk/assessments/products/lucid-cops/

- Auditory memory
- Sequencing skills

Then work out what strategies you need to put in place to support those gaps – there are loads of fun games that can be given to play at home that will help develop those parts of the working memory.

Please don't use dyslexia as an excuse for failure. If a child has a genuine barrier to learning, do everything you can to find out what it is so that it can be overcome or accepted.

AVOID REPEATING NONSENSICAL TARGETS

Targets should never exist for target's sake. If you are giving parents a target for reports, make it SMART. And NEVER give one related to handwriting! Check to see what targets were given last time. If you're giving them the same target, you're wasting your time. However, if you give them a target that you know you'll cover in school at some point, then the child is more likely to achieve it.

S - Specific
M - Measurable
A - Achievable
R - Realistic
T - Timed

I once decided to check a child's previous report targets before setting new ones. For five years their target had been "improve your handwriting". Clearly, it hadn't worked! Parents were disengaged and believed each teacher who had repeated the target was either lazy or absolving themselves of responsibility by passing the task to them.

I set them a new target: write the letter 'a' as though it was the best letter in the alphabet and deserved to be treated with more respect. As soon as it looks good, we'll move on to 'e'.

By focusing on one letter, the parents got on board. I monitored it in the classroom too. And by mastering the vowels, other letters began to change shape automatically.

Check out the *Target Ladders* books published by LDA[9] for more pre-written and incredible targets complete with matching ideas for support. These books literally transformed my provision for special needs and saw significant, targeted improvements for the children involved.

BLACK AND WHITE WORKSHEETS CAN CAUSE VISUAL STRESS

Have you ever noticed some children always seem to have

---

9 https://www.ldalearning.com/product/cognition-and-learning/dyslexia-and-literacy/teaching-resources/target-ladders-dyslexia-book/aamt12584

bags under their eyes? Or struggle to focus on their work? It could be that they are suffering from visual stress. Screening children at around Year 3 is highly recommended. We identified anyone whose reading was below age expectations in reading. We would then ask them to read various texts written in black on white paper and carefully ask them what they could see. Nobody was led, but often children would say things like "I can see spots on the page" or "The letters kind of move". This is the result of the same strobing effect we sometimes see on TV with striped tops.

We then put a coloured overlay over the text. Often, the children would look absolutely shocked as the movement stopped! At this point, we would refer them to an optician for a formal diagnosis, who would identify which colour was best for that child.

USE FAVOURITE COLOURS FOR SPECIAL OCCASIONS

One year, I was fortunate enough to have an incredibly bright autistic mathematician. His autism meant staying focused and communicating his knowledge was tricky, despite having a 1-1 teaching assistant to support him in maths lessons. Completing tests was particularly tricky. One day, I discovered his favourite colour was yellow. I decided to photocopy his test onto yellow paper. He was VERY happy to complete it and proved he was supposed to be in the top group.

The following year, the message about the yellow paper became muddied, despite me being clear in the transition. They decided to make ALL of his worksheets yellow so that they'd ALL appeal more. A logical step for any other child, but not for this one. This led to a distinct dislike of tests again as they weren't special. His results dropped.

CHOOSE AN INTERN

Children with ADHD often come with a negative reputation. The extra energy required to manage them can lead to a lower quality relationship with the teacher. My strategy to combat this was to make the child with ADHD use their energy in productive ways. They became my intern/helper/teaching assistant.

- Be ready to run after a student
- Never put your guard down
- Block slaps and thrown toys
- Smile often
- Keep a good attitude
- Show interest in the student
- Have a good sense of humour
- Listen to the student as they talk to you
- Don't take anything mean that is said personally

- Have a patient heart
- Show love in action
- Do not be phased by toilet accidents
- Speak kindly
- Give boundaries
- Front load student with work expectations
- Work hard
- Don't forget to collect data and progress for each student
- Teach with enthusiasm

Angela Baker
(TA in a Special Needs school)

10

Parents

MAKE PARENTS EVENINGS POSITIVE

There are some children that you want to moan about. But remember, every teacher ever will have made the same moans. Instead, talk about what you are putting in place to support the problems:

YOUR CHILD'S HANDWRITING IS BAD
We noticed that your child's handwriting wasn't great, so we put daily exercises in place to develop muscle strength and coordination. Here is a pack you can try at home. Once you've finished it, we'll make up another.

YOUR CHILD HAS FAILED TO LEARN THEIR TIMES TABLES.
We noticed that your child struggles with their times tables. Why not buy one of those cheap huge posters with the tables on and stick it somewhere. Every time they show they've learnt one of the calculations, cut it off the poster or cross it out. Eventually there will be nothing left to learn.

CASE STUDY

A child with a bad reputation joined my class. He bullied other children. He was constantly on a behaviour chart. Parents had been called and were supportive but had no ideas, as nothing seemed to have an effect. I decided to give him a clean slate. He started in my class, and very quickly made himself known. He shouted out a few times. Throughout that first week, we focused on creating a class community and having a supportive ethos. He took that on board. I was nothing but positive, gently reminding him of how this year was different and that in our class everyone was good.

Then I made him my intern. I get sore throats very easily due to an acid reflux problem, so I drink a lot when I'm teaching. Every time I needed a drink, I'd send him to top up my glass from the water fountain outside. Every day he did the register, choosing someone sensible to help him (we got over the fact he always took the same friend by allowing him to choose the same person every Friday so long as he picked other people for the rest of the week).

There were times when I could see him getting restless as he worked, so I'd quickly go over and ask for a drink. Several full glasses were subtly poured down the sink to enable this to happen!

I knew I'd won when I walked up to him one day and asked him to get me a drink and he asked if I could choose somebody else because he wanted to get his work done.

YOUR CHILD'S BEHAVIOUR IS DISTRACTING EVERYBODY ELSE
We noticed that your child gets easily distracted, so we've put a three-strike system in place/asked for a referral from the behaviour unit/provided a fiddle toy/provided a wobble cushion to keep them focused. What strategies do you use at home? Would you appreciate a further conversation about supporting behaviour with our parent support advisor?

In all of these examples, I have not hidden the fact that there is a problem. However, I have focused on the solution rather than absolving myself of all responsibility.

START PARENT'S EVENINGS WITH A QUESTION

This one is easy – always start with the following script:

> *"Welcome – thank you so much for coming. I guess the best place to start is: 'Do you have any questions?'"*

This sounds like the thing you'd say last, but it actually helps control the time you spend with each parent surprisingly efficiently. Rather than start with a spiel that might not interest the parent at all, you begin by discovering the exact topic that they have come to discuss.

There is nothing worse than getting to the end of your spiel, then asking the question and discovering that it's going to take another ten minutes to unravel the answer.

And if they genuinely don't want to know anything specific, focus on the positives and strategies for success, finishing early where possible so you can give more time to parents who might be harder to deal with.

PARTNER WITH THE PARENTS

For the time you have their child in your class, you are just one major influence on their life. The parents are another huge influence. Always use the language of 'partnering' and 'working alongside'.

Remember that when a child goes home, they take with them a narrative about your class. But they also collect a narrative from their parent(s). If the child has had a bad day, the parent (who is only aware of part of the picture) might say all the things you should have done as a teacher, no matter how unrealistic those expectations would be. This will introduce an invisible barrier between you and the child.

However, if the parents know you are approachable, then they will simply say "let's speak to your teacher tomorrow" or "I'll send them a quick email and see if we can help."

CASE STUDY

She sat opposite me looking nervous. Her 10-year-old child was not academically able and had a reputation for poor behaviour. In the first few months I had worked hard trying to get to identify and put strategies in place to overcome his barriers to learning.

I sat, acknowledging that his handwriting wasn't great but saying that we'd given him daily muscle development activities and gave her some games to play at home. I explained that, although he did get distracted, the strategies I had been using were working and he was beginning to want to show me what he had achieved.

I thanked her for being patient with me as I got to know her son, explaining that I was taking full responsibility for her son's behaviour and academic progress and that I enjoyed working with him because I could see his potential.

It was at that point she burst into tears. Confused, I asked what was wrong. She explained that in 5 years of schooling she had never experienced a positive parents evening. Every encounter with a teacher had been negative, and she had received countless reminders that she had failed as a parent.

I'd pointed out all the same problems other teachers had identified – things that she had been told year after year with no change – but I worded it positively and proactively. She was totally on my side after that, and as a result, her son made exceptional progress, both academically and emotionally that year.

I also want to add that I do not blame the other teachers for this parent's experience. And I don't believe that they had never said anything positive. However, in this moment, this parent's perception was that this had been a wholly positive evening having as many negatives pointed out as on previous occasions.

Now the parent is on your side. There is no barrier. And as a team you can support the academic and emotional welfare of every child in your class.

EMAIL IS A VALUABLE TOOL

This is another potentially controversial one. Very early on in my career, when sharing your professional email was considered taboo, I gave mine out to every parent and encouraged them to contact me. I explained that I would not respond to emails outside of normal working hours (although I often did if I was working late at home marking or preparing lessons).

Having the parents' comments BEFORE they came to visit was hugely helpful. Often, a quick email back would resolve their issue and save them trying to talk to me the next day. On other occasions, it allowed me to speak to the relevant people or get the evidence I needed to provide a solid response. This increased the parent's confidence in my ability and did wonders for my reputation.

But more importantly, it meant that stress didn't bubble up in the parents.

PARENTS ARE RESOURCES

Get to know your parents – ask the children what their parents do for a living. You never know who you have! I've taken advantage of many of their skills to enhance their own child's educational experience. To list just a few...

- One dad was a doctor who specialised in ears – he gave the most accurate and exciting lessons on ears and how sound works using equipment from his job
- One family realised one of our topics was going to be India, so filmed a documentary while on holiday there during the summer holidays in preparation
- One grandparent visited annually to speak about her Jewish faith – when I moved from one school to another, I took her with me!
- A mother who had once been a concert violinist became an inspirational sensation

Of course, some parents sound good but don't have the ability to transfer their knowledge to the classroom. Make sure you screen people where possible. Never promise to use someone every year. Only invite back once you've experienced a successful lesson.

Similarly, you may have some parents you'd rather not help out with every school trip. If you know which parents are most effective in those situations, and can invite them personally, then you can explain to other parents that you already have enough this time. Keep parent interactions positive and your life will be much easier.

CASE STUDY

I still remember one parent who would email me angrily, then come in the next day to apologise! I got used to ignoring the first email, knowing that I could resolve the issue the next day easily. It turned out that the parent was struggling at home, and her ability to email her stress transformed her relationship with the school. Instead of turning up angry, she turned up apologetic, and from there we could have a constructive conversation.

On that note, remember that when somebody writes something in an email, you can't see their face. It is impersonal. Do not take anything personally. Patiently discuss issues, and always reply in a professional manner, sending a copy to your line manager when needed.

11

Secondary Transition

YOU WON'T NEED IT FOR SECONDARY SCHOOL

Never imagine that your experience of Secondary School is the same as your pupil's experience will be. I worked in Primary teaching for years before switching to the maths department of a Secondary School. Many of the formal written methods of calculation that I had been encouraging my class to learn because they'd 'need it for Secondary School' had been replaced by the much easier grid method or other more visual tools.

Similarly, phrases like "they won't tolerate that in Secondary School" were complete nonsense. Teachers working in the next phase of education have no magic wand that automatically makes everybody behave. They have the same targets, same demands, same pressures that Primary School teachers have.

They are also human.

If anything, we do a disservice to them by using them as a threat. Because when the 'threat' turns out to be false, it just gives pupils their first reason to misbehave.

Instead, we should be talking about 'fresh starts', 'first impressions' and 'new opportunities.' Moving to Secondary School is a chance for children to set up new habits of learning, work out how to communicate and get along with many different teachers, and settle into a very new environment/ culture for the first time. If we prepared them properly for this amazing opportunity by making it sound good, instead of using it as a weak threat, I'm sure they'd enjoy the transition process that much more.

BE FRIENDS WITH YOUR LOCAL SECONDARY

If you end up in years 5 or 6, you'll become more aware of secondary schools. Become friends with them. They have resources that you don't have. Over the course of one year, my Year 5s experienced a Christmas Science show, used tech skills to produce their own fridge magnets and massive posters, took part in maths competitions and got to conduct science experiments of their own, dissecting flowers, analysing rock samples and using Bunsen burners! I became friends with the staff at our partner school, especially the member of staff responsible for liaison. They ended up providing tech support one morning a week, helped us transform our library system by cataloguing every single book and were an invaluable source of information.

DON'T CLAIM TO KNOW MORE THAN YOU DO

Parents often ask about local schools and whether you have any recommendations. In these situations, it would be easy to answer the question based on your own experiences with those schools. But unless you're the parent to a teenager, you're unlikely to have an accurate picture of what is going on. Be honest. Encourage parents to do their research. And if you're asked about the appropriateness of grammar school education, don't raise expectations too high. Be realistic. Again, encourage them to do their research, to try some of the practise tests and decide whether the approach to learning suits their child.

From a personal point of view, I had to pick one of three schools for my son. There were two local secondary schools within our catchment as well as one grammar. My son is not academic – he is artistic. The grammar school was ruled out. Looking at the work on display and the homework policies, it was clear that Secondary B was better suited than Secondary A. In the end, the deciding factor was his girlfriend. She chose Secondary A. It was more important that he was happy socially than academically, so we went with his decision. He did well, raised his game and adapted to the school well. If we had been upset, we knew we could transfer him. We never felt the need.

12

Reputation Makers

MAGIC TRICKS

You'd be amazed at how many pupils love a bit of magic, and it's really easy to learn a few very simple tricks. I enjoy the supposed mind reading tricks that require very little effort:

Write the word 'what' on a piece of paper.

Me: I bet I know what you're thinking?

Them: What?

Me: Reveals the word 'what'

Me: Think of an odd number between 1 and 10 [quietly write the number 7]

Them: 7 [90% of people pick 7]

Me: Reveal the number 7

The two other tricks I usually do are classics. I ask them to repeat the number 6 a few times while secretly writing the word 'carrot' – ask them to name a vegetable and they'll pick carrot 90% of the time. The same works with asking for tools – they'll usually pick a hammer.

I've also learned very simple card tricks or basic magic tricks from various online guides – nothing complicated and nothing requiring much practice. They nearly always get a good reaction and help build my reputation for memorable lessons.

Why bother with stunts and tricks? Because the best learners ask questions – and magic leads us to ask the question 'how' and think beyond our realm of understanding. Magic can lead us to a place of awe and wonder – both emotional experiences that have drained out of schools by tired teachers trying their best to cram in a stuffed curriculum.

BE AN INFLUENCER

For several years, I carried a pebble in my pocket. It reminded me that I will never know where my influence ends. The impact that I have as a teacher – and the impact you will have – is immeasurable. There will be memories formed and experiences that change the lives of the pupils you teach. And on that note...

GUERRILLA MUSIC

Credit for this idea has to go to a colleague, and I have no idea whether it was his or something he discovered online. But it's so good, it's worth mentioning! If this is your idea, I apologise in advance and give you full credit. For one week, musicians were invited to interrupt lessons and perform for pupils. We had break time shows and assemblies filled with incredible rhythms. It led to a huge boost in pupils taking up music lessons, which in turn resulted in our first school orchestra! Musicians were either music teachers or parents who happened to play. If a teachers' door was left open, then it was in invitation to be interrupted.

BE FRIENDS WITH THE OFFICE STAFF

The staff who work in the office are your friends. Recognise that they are also busy doing jobs you don't even realise exist. They are the frontline for parents and protect you from extra workload. They do more than you can imagine. Ask how they are! Have a solid working relationship with them. Thank them! Be grateful for what they do. If you go over and above to help them, they'll go over and above to help you.

MANAGING BUDGETS TO THE PENNY

Some schools require teachers to put in a budget request for their subject area of responsibility. Every budget I ever requested I received in full. After a few years of hearing how other teachers had been turned down for funding, I approached the Headteacher and asked why. The answer was simple – she recognised that, because I was requesting amounts to the exact penny, I had done my research. I know exactly how much everything was going to cost and therefore she could trust that my request would be accurate.

What she didn't know is that I would use one of the biggest suppliers to get the initial prices and then I would challenge myself to find cheaper prices elsewhere so that I had spare money to spend on extra resources! The important thing was that I was fully aware of the budget.

CASE STUDY

You never know what impact you're going to have. Several years ago, early in my career, I used a magic trick in a French lesson. One of the people who saw me became so captivated in magic that before a decade had passed, they had worked their way up the ranks and actually performed magic at Las Vegas! He didn't need a word of French that I'd taught, but that simple trick changed his life.

More recently, I used a card trick in a maths lesson with a Secondary pupil. A week later, he was back with his own deck of cards ready to impress. This silent teenager had discovered something that fascinated him and I'm sure it will become a useful party trick for years to come...

LEARN A NEW SKILL

I'm stealing this one from my all-time favourite book for teachers: *Inspirational Teachers Inspirational Learners* by Will Ryan[10]. It's a must-read for anyone wanting to be a teacher. In fact, if you've picked my book up in a shop or library and are wondering whether to buy it and have glanced at this paragraph, put my book back and buy Will Ryan's! It's that good!

Anyway...

Ask the school to nominate something for you to learn. Then, for a year, actively demonstrate yourself learning. Let the school watch your progress – see you fail and overcome challenges. I ended up learning how to solve a Rubik's cube, how to catch (yes, I'm that bad at sports) and how to juggle as a result of this personal challenge. By modelling that you are a learner and modelling how to behave when you're finding things tough, you'll be a really positive example. Even better, you get to learn something new.

THE RANDOM ROUND OF APPLAUSE

I like putting on a show. It got to the point where I could get a round of applause for deciding to use a different pen, or for removing my coat.

---

10 https://www.amazon.co.uk/Inspirational-Teachers-Learners-Creativity-Curriculum/dp/1845904435

CASE STUDY

This is an unusual case study. It's more like an homage to my own teachers. They each formed memories that stuck with me. Thank you to:

- Mrs Fewing (Year 1), who saw my potential and encouraged me in maths

- Mrs Goodworth (Year 2); her strict persona was exactly what we needed during the storms

- Mrs Baldwin (Year 3); I still remember story time vividly

- Mrs Newall (Year 4), who inspired me to become a teacher

- Mr Alford (Year 5) – I may have hidden in the cupboard every time bus stop division came up, but he saw something in me and sat me with various pupils to be a positive influence on them

- Mrs Passmore (Year 6) who recently received a copy of my first book and made a point of writing to me. Her words of encouragement meant the world!

- And further into Secondary School, Mr Mason gets special mention, because he was the one who boosted my maths confidence again. My teaching degree specialism ended up being maths because of him, and my most recent work in schools has been based on his methods.

In fact, there was one GCSE skill (solving quadratic equations) that I'd totally forgotten when I began tutoring secondary maths pupils. After a week of panicking about the topic I was supposed to be teaching, I prayed and had one last sleep. I had a dream that night. I was back in his class. He re-taught me the method he had used. When I woke up, I remembered everything and have been teaching it ever since!!! The memory of his lesson was stored in my mind and came just when I needed (either that or, if you believe it, he decided to visit me from beyond the grave when I needed it most – and no, I have no idea if he's still alive or not!)

You might be wondering why this is a top tip?

Well, some lessons are just boring. No matter what I do, I can't find the fun angle and there are moments when I see that class isn't focusing. Maybe my opening input was too long because they didn't understand something and I had to cover it more, or maybe it's just one of those days. Who knows.

But in that moment, I turn to write something on the board, pick up a pen and announce in a dramatic voice:

"No, I am NOT going to use the black pen. Today, ladies and gentlemen, I am going to use............. THE BLUE PEN!"

I can normally get some "oooo's" and "aaaah's" or a round of applause if I build it correctly. This momentary break in routine reinvigorates the most boring of lessons.

START THE UNIT WITH A BANG

You're probably getting the idea by now that I like to take advantage of children's imaginations. From walks in the local park searching for Gruffalo clues to immersive classroom experiences, I think these moments make memories that last beyond the curriculum.

TRY TEACHING WITHOUT TALKING

I suffer from sore throats. All of the time. So many of my strategies have come from not being able to just raise my voice above the noise. But what happens when my voice is gone completely? Actually, my class understands me so well that I don't even need to speak.

CASE STUDY

Ofsted was on the prowl, going from room to room, and my voice had all but given up. I was dreading the moment that they came in and saw me unable to teach. I decided to rest my voice and teach through mime. My Year 3 class were all ready to engage.

I picked up four plastic fraction apples. I mimed eating one. I mimed not liking the taste and being annoyed at the fact it was plastic. I picked up the next apple – one that split in two. I mimed a karate chop and ended up with one half in each hand. I looked from one to the other. One child shouted "half" and I nodded enthusiastically at them. I returned to the whole apple. The children, now getting the idea, said "whole".

I repeated the process for quarters and thirds. I even compared the halves and quarters effectively, with the children coming up with all the language. I didn't say a word. I then put my finger to my lips and signalled them to come closer.

I whispered, "Activities are on the table." The entire class quietly rose from their places and were able to complete everything. I spoke a total of 5 words: activities are on the table.

CASE STUDY

60 Year 5 children entered the drama hall and sat facing a row of tables. At one end were various fruits, each one a scale representation of a planet. There was also an umbrella (one-eighth of the sun). In silence, I opened the umbrella. The entire year group watched in silence, trying to work out what was going on. Then, I picked up a fruit and placed it on the table. Again, I went back and picked up another piece of fruit. I continued until all eight pieces of fruit were spread out on the table.

Somebody whispered, "it's the planets." A teacher observing said, "well done," followed by "oops." But it didn't matter – my own enthusiastic nodding said exactly the same thing.

I paused to look at the fruits, frowned, then swapped two of them. I nodded with a smile on my face. We had been studying the planets, so they all had some idea of what we were looking at. They began to put their hands up to make suggestions (one had shouted out, but I'd mimed a hand up and they all joined in the game). Fruit by fruit we rearranged everything until it was in the correct order. The only whispers I heard were productive noise – conversations trying to remember key facts about the planets or attempting to recall mnemonics for their order.

Once it was correct, I stood back looking satisfied. I then began to explain out loud some bonus facts that they'd missed or corrected a few misconceptions they'd overheard. I congratulated the problem-solving techniques they'd used and the logical conclusions they'd arrived at.

When they returned to class, they now had some sort of context for how much bigger and smaller the planets were. Our ➜

➔ provided objectives had seemed weighty and totally out of context – there was no way these children would remember the relative sizes of the planets in a few months. But now, there was a chance they had a memory that would lay the foundations for future study...

And in case you want to repeat this science activity yourself: Mercury was a raisin, Venus and Earth were cherry tomatoes, Mars was a blueberry, Jupiter was a watermelon, Saturn was a large grapefruit, Uranus was an apple and Neptune was an orange. Enjoy!

14

The Final Tip

ABANDON GROWTH MINDSET, BRAIN GYM AND OTHER NONSENSE FADS

This is a personal annoyance. I got repeatedly frustrated by initiatives being introduced that had no educational benefit or no researched evidence to back them up. Brain gym – the idea that by doing some weird movements we can activate both sides of our brain and get them working in harmony – was disproved but not before it was adopted by almost every classroom in the country. The latest fad appears to be a misinterpretation of growth mindset – the idea that if you just try, you can overcome anything. This is a huge distortion of the original research, twisted to make all teachers and children feel like failures because they *should* be able to achieve anything.

It is true that if a child has a negative attitude towards work, they won't achieve their best. But having a positive attitude won't help them achieve anything and telling them that is dangerous. We have a generation coming through that believes that anything is possible if they set their mind to it. Social media is full of inspirational messages based on wishy-washy dreams, encouraging them to reach for the stars, and yet we have a generation on antidepressants, struggling to match their dreams with reality. We also have people coming out of university with a level of arrogance previously unseen, believing that those with experience have nothing to contribute to the conversation, or believing that their qualification makes them fully skilled for leadership. This leads to division.

Instead, I want to suggest something else.

We need to encourage children to get excited about the world around them, to pose questions but also to pause in wonder. We need to explain to them the importance of life-long learning, of journeying with people through difficulties, of recognising the benefits of experience.

There's a story I love where two generations are in the same room. The older generation is encouraged to hold the hand of one of the younger generation and lead them around the room. This is supposed to signify that we should be investing in the younger generation, passing on the benefits of our experience. They were then encouraged to swap places. The younger generation also had benefits – maybe fresh approaches and viewpoints that could be integrated into current practice. In other words, there was equal respect for what each generation brought to the deal.

CASE STUDY

In one English unit, we were going to be writing letters home to England from Egypt describing the artefacts we had discovered in various digs. I was one of two classes in the same year group teaching the same lesson at the same time. We both decided we would print off pictures of artefacts and children would try and guess what they were.

In the class next door, the children were each given one picture. They had to write on their whiteboard what they thought it was, then share with a partner to see if they agreed. Then, the class finished by sharing their findings in an orderly way.

In my class, we started outside the classroom. I explained that we'd just found the entrance to a long-lost Egyptian tomb filled with incredible artefacts. We had to enter very quietly, sneaking in so that we didn't disturb the old ruins. When they entered, the tables had the same pictures of artefacts scattered around. They all wandered around the class, taking in ALL of the pictures. On my signal, they crept to their own seats and started to share what they had seen with their partners. They posed questions that needed answering. Then they picked a picture from their own table and began to describe what it was.

You can imagine that there was a different level of excitement in each class. In the first class, children wrote a sentence or two factually describing what they saw. In my class, they wrote a paragraph filled with emotive language. There was nothing wrong with the approach next door, and the calm controlled atmosphere led to beautifully presented books filled with accurate sentences. My books weren't as neat, and there were a few more mistakes to correct, so you have to find the right balance.

Let's be realistic with our classes. Let's praise their strengths, look for opportunities for their characters to grow and celebrate the fact that each class is a united community. If we do this, society will gradually be transformed by a generation keen to include others using positive language, patience and understanding.

IF YOU DECIDE TO LEAVE THE CLASSROOM

And should you ever decide to leave teaching and work elsewhere, you'll realise a few things about the outside world. I gave these tips to a friend who was leaving the classroom and she recommended I share them here too:

1. Nobody is as efficient as people that work in schools – be patient
2. Nobody is as busy as people that work in schools – it's okay to slow down
3. Nobody is as judged as people that work in schools – don't be so hard on yourself
4. Nobody realises how hard teachers work – don't show your colleagues up
5. Nobody realises how rewarding teaching can be – don't forget to look back with fond memories

I will admit, I left the classroom for a season and learned these things the hard way. I was spending too much time outside of the classroom running training for current and future teachers and decided it was unfair on my character-filled class to juggle both roles. But I missed it so much I ended up returning in a more balanced capacity! These final top tips for survival outside were learned the hard way as I began to realise that the pace of life I had believed was normal when working as a teacher was anything but.

Another friend of mine – someone who had started as a volunteer, then completed his teacher training in my year group, then worked his way up to be a nationally recognised teacher – recently stepped out of the classroom to work for the union full time. He could see the impact this pressure was having on staff and children alike and chose to devote his time to campaigning for change.

Whether you stay in the system or step out, know that being a teacher is one of the most important, rewarding experiences you will ever have. You will literally change the lives of those you work with, giving them memories that will last a lifetime and shape their future.

Thank you for your time. Thank you for your energy. Thank you for going above and beyond.

Thank you for being a teacher.

Printed in Great Britain
by Amazon